THE SCORE AND TEN

SIMONNE FERGUSON

 FriesenPress

One Printers Way
Altona, MB R0G 0B0
Canada

www.friesenpress.com

ISBN
978-1-03-913729-5 (Hardcover)
978-1-03-913728-8 (Paperback)
978-1-03-913730-1 (eBook)

1. BIOGRAPHY & AUTOBIOGRAPHY, PERSONAL MEMOIRS

Distributed to the trade by The Ingram Book Company

DEDICATION

To the great-grandchildren:
Billy, Addie, Camryn, Ali, Aiden, and Mason.

"Life is either a daring adventure or nothing at all." Helen Keller

TABLE OF CONTENTS

CHAPTER 1
INTRODUCTION:
SOMETIME IN 1922

Three-year-old Sheila quietly slipped out of bed.

It was dark in the small room she shared with her four older sisters. Agnes and Nora were softly snoring in their bed, and Kathleen and Eileen were sprawled across the bed Sheila shared with them, having pushed her so far to the edge she'd woken up. It was then she heard voices in the kitchen below. She tiptoed carefully to the door to listen, trying not to wake the others, and in the pre-dawn chill, crept shivering half way down the stairs to investigate further.

Her mother Nellie was standing over the large Victorian cooking range, the fire warming the kitchen and reflecting off a pot hanging from a hook above it. It was the only light in the room, but Sheila could still see a man sitting at the table with a cup of tea and some toast and jam in front of him. For a moment she was about to call out, thinking this was her father William returned unexpectedly from working away in Ireland, but then realized he didn't look the same at all. The tired-looking stranger had on a ragged coat and worn black boots, as if he had either just arrived or was about to rush out.

Sheila had a child's sense there was something wrong with what she was seeing, something she didn't understand, and she knew she shouldn't make any noise to alert to her mother she was there. She very quietly crawled back up to the bedroom, taking care to avoid the creaky step, her back to the wall of the stairwell for stability. She slid back under the bedcovers into the warmth and security of her sisters' bodies and quickly fell back to sleep.

The next morning, the kitchen was filled with the usual noise and boisterous energy of her eight brothers and sisters as they rushed through their bowls of porridge and hastily gulped down their tea. "Don't forget to take that note to the Sisters," Nellie instructed as they shoved and pushed each other out the door. "And Bill and Kevin, stop in at the butcher's for those soup bones on your way home. And tuck in your shirts!!"

"Okay Ma, cheerio!" they called back as they ran down Richmond Street to school. "See you later."

It was only then, as quiet finally settled over the house again, that Sheila could get her mother's attention for a few moments. "Mama, who was the man here last night? In the kitchen with you? Drinking tea?"

Nellie stopped what she was doing and stood absolutely still for a moment, then took a deep breath and wiped her hands on her apron. She looked at little Sheila's eager face, filled with curiosity, and forced a smile. "No no, Sheila!" she said. "Where did you ever get such an idea!? There was no man here. And you'd better not be telling tales like that to anyone, my little chatterbox, or people will think there's something not proper in this house."

And the nosy English neighbours will figure out pretty quickly that we're helping out the IRA rebels passing through, Nellie thought to herself for the hundredth time, *and then what will we do?*

CHAPTER 2
BEING IRISH:
THE TURN OF THE 20TH CENTURY

Sheila's father, William Patrick O'Carroll, was born in the small village of Abbeyleix, Ireland, in November 1873, the son of William O'Carroll and Mary Ann Murphy, poor tenant farmers on the estate of the English viscount De Vesci, as had been their parents and the parents before them. The O'Carrolls, like most of the Irish, did not have much hope of ever owning land or being more than labourers for someone else. For many centuries, Irish land was owned and managed by the British aristocracy. The Irish worked for them but owned little and were considered second class citizens in their own country; they had no power to control its destiny. By all accounts, the generations of De Vescis weren't bad landlords in comparison to others in Ireland, and made sure their workers were treated fairly. They improved the village of Abbeyleix, even building a new Boys' School in 1884 when William was ten.

The De Vescis also started a carpet factory to provide employment for the villagers and, notably, some of its products ended up on the Titanic.

William and all of his six siblings left Ireland to find meaningful work elsewhere and ended up dispersed around the world. Abbeyleix was well situated for leaving, as it was positioned halfway between Cork in the south and Dublin in the east, on the main road between the two cities. It was easy to go in one direction or the other, Cork if you were going to Canada or the USA, Dublin if you were going to England. William went to England. His older brother Thomas went to South Africa, and was never heard from again. His sisters Polly, Frances, and Mary Theresa emigrated to the USA around the turn of the 20th century and became maids in wealthy households in New York City. His sister Bridget (Bridie) went to England first and then on across the Atlantic to America. It was the quintessential story of the Irish since the potato famine. Ireland's biggest export was its people.

By contrast, Sheila's mother Nellie Hollick came from entirely different circumstances: she was born in 1882 to a financially secure, middle-class English couple living in the Midlands. Nellie's father Richard Hollick was a noted pharmacist in Birmingham, a respected and influential member of the community, a city councillor, and a renowned stamp collector and chess player. He was also a staunch member of the Conservative Party and a loyal church-going Protestant. His wife, Sarah Jane Leuttit, was originally from the Orkney Islands in Scotland, and had met Richard, nine years her senior, when he was visiting there on a vacation. That he was able to travel for pleasure and enjoy a holiday hallmarked his comfortable lifestyle.

Shortly after meeting Richard Hollick, young Sarah Jane came south to Birmingham as a guest of the renowned Spiritualist Thomas Colley. At the time, Spiritualism was a fad among the middle and upper classes, who believed that the dead could communicate with the living in various ways. It was a movement particularly attractive to women, including Sarah Jane. A woman's life was very constrained in the Victorian period, but this was an acceptable way of adding a little excitement to her otherwise restricted options. Sarah Jane's friend Thomas Colley was a leader in the field; he claimed that the ghostly shapes appearing in his photographs were in fact spirits visible only to

4

the camera. His friend, Sir Arthur Conan Doyle, creator of Sherlock Holmes, and the poet Elizabeth Barrett Browning were also believers, and even Queen Victoria participated in séances. Teenage Sarah Jane was intrigued. It was on this trip that Richard Hollick successfully pursued his courtship of her, and not long after they were married. Sarah Jane was only nineteen years old when their daughter Nellie was born.

Unlike the big Catholic family William O'Carroll came from, Nellie Hollick had only one sibling, a younger brother named Gilbert.

The distinctions between William's opportunities in life and Nellie's were truly significant. They were on opposite sides of what, at the time, was often an insurmountable social, political, and religious wall. The likelihood was indeed slim that a poor Irish Catholic working man might marry a privileged English Protestant woman at the end of the 19th century. The courtship and romance of Sheila's parents William O'Carroll and Nellie Hollick defied social expectations and is the stuff of novels.

William had left Ireland in the late 1800s and lived for a time with his older sister Bridie in Birmingham. Bridie was working for the Hollick family as a domestic servant, a very typical Irish maid in a comfortable middle class English home. When the Hollicks needed someone to care for their horses, Bridie recommended her newly arrived brother.

"Excuse me, Mr. Hollick, sir," she said with a slight dip of one knee. "I'm wondering if you'd like to meet my brother William? He's lots of experience with the horses on Viscount De Vesci's estate back in the old country." William was hired.

Inevitably, William would come to meet Nellie, Richard's daughter. She was a bright, educated, and lively young woman in her late teens with strong opinions. She often disagreed with the confining Victorian worldview of her father. She followed the current events and political movements of the day in the newspapers, reading about the troubles in Ireland, suffrage for women, and the Boer War.

Nellie had a bicycle, unusual for a woman at the turn of the century and a clear sign that she was independently minded and prepared to test the limits of social convention. One day in mid-May, 1900, she decorated her bicycle spokes with red and blue ribbons to celebrate Britain's victory over the Boers at the long-fought battle in the little South African town of Mafeking. After a seven-month siege, the village was finally taken back from the Boers, leading to great celebrations in Britain. Flags waved, people cheered in the streets, and factory sirens tooted. Tucking her long skirt safely under her seat, Nellie proudly rode her decorated bicycle around Birmingham, a happy young Englishwoman enjoying the great victory.

Employee William found the boss's daughter's blatant display of English patriotism offensive, thinking of his brother Thomas in South Africa and of the long English oppression of his own country. As interested and informed of world events as Nellie was, William saw them from a different point of view. He was appalled with the reports of Britain's poor treatment of the Black population in Africa. It was all too similar to the situation in Ireland.

"You arrogant English!" he snapped at her when she deposited her bicycle at the stables for him to put away after the celebration. "You think you have the right to trample on anyone in the world and do whatever you want, don't ye?" Nellie was taken aback by the outburst from the handsome Irishman working for her father. She looked at his rolled up sleeves and his greasy hands. "Whatever are you talking about?" she said. "England just won an important battle!"

"England is it? Do you have any idea how many Irishmen died fight-ing for *your* Queen Victoria? She's not *my* queen," he said, wiping away the rivulets of sweat running from under his cap. "Just so you can take over more land from more poor working people in another country? We're all just your slaves as far as you English are concerned".

"How dare you!" Nellie replied imperiously, her hands on her hips, but as she turned and walked away she remembered the things she had been reading and the discomfort she'd felt at some of the stories about England's handling of the war. She had already begun to question her religious affiliation with the Church of England, and was considering converting to the Catholic church, and now she began to feel uncomfortable about the longstanding fight over Ireland.

This was the first of their many arguments, not just about the Boer War, but also about politics, religion and social class. Sparks flew—in more ways than one. The "bicycle ribbon incident" sparked a relationship that lasted most of the next six decades.

Nellie's father Richard Hollick was deeply disturbed by his only daughter's growing relationship with the Irish groom. It was an affront to his political views and his social standing.

"You CANNOT do this!" he bellowed, pacing his well-appointed Victorian parlour when she told him her plans. "I FORBID IT!"

"Do you care nothing of my humiliation at the Club? How can I hold my head up in church if you do this? What will the Vicar think?" he ranted. "It's bad enough that you've been seen sneaking into the Catholic church, but now you're carrying on with the man who mucks out our horses?" He was livid.

Nellie stood as tall as her five foot stature would allow, bravely looking up at her father. "He's a good, decent man," she said calmly. "You know I don't share your old-fashioned views on the Irish or religion. I love William and I'm going to marry him. I don't really care what you think."

Richard Hollick was both stunned and saddened by his young daughter's defiance. "If you go through with this," he said, "then you are no longer my daughter."

Nellie was undeterred, and eventually, she and William married in November 1905. She was twenty-three years old when she left the social acceptance of her father's comfortable home and community status to make a life with her charming Irishman, nine years her senior. Indeed, her father disowned her as he had promised to do. It was not until the death of Nellie's first child that Richard Hollick began to soften even a little and to speak to his daughter again.

William and Nellie O'Carroll continued to live in Birmingham, where he worked as a salesman for a brewery, making deliveries in a pony and cart, but somehow he found the time and means to attend the Birmingham Technical Institute. He became a skilled tool and die maker. Their first child, Gerald, was born very soon after they married, but died within a few weeks from pneumonia. A second child, Mary Agnes, came along in October 1906. Many more children followed, like stair steps. Two years later came Nora, and twenty-one months after that, Kevin arrived. In 1909, the O'Carrolls moved into a little house at 122 Richmond Street in the central part of Coventry when new working class homes were being built there. It was a very modest, typical row house: two rooms up and two rooms down. It didn't take long to fill the house: Kathleen arrived in 1913, then Bill in 1914, Eileen in 1915, Bernard in 1916, and Patrick in 1917.

On February 12th, 1919, three months after the Armistice ended the brutal First World War, and in the midst of the devastating Spanish Flu pandemic, little Sheila O'Carroll made her debut. She was delivered at home in her parents' bed. It was a particularly cold February that year, and a huge dump of snow had hit the Midlands a week or so earlier, with temperatures below normal. Her oldest sister Agnes rounded up the youngsters and got them out of the way, bundling them up and taking them to play in the cold street until the noise and mess of childbirth was over. Just three weeks before Sheila was born, Ireland had declared independence from Britain and proclaimed itself the Irish Republic. William was elated. In 1918, a year before Sheila was born, women over the age of thirty were given the right to vote, making Nellie happy too.

The time was both auspicious and unsettled. The world was changing rapidly and dramatically.

The Irish Catholic tradition was to name each child after a saint, but Sheila's parents were running out of choices when she arrived. They wanted to give her the old Irish name of Sheila, meaning heavenly, but it was not a saint's name. The first child in the family, the only one who didn't survive, was named after St. Gerald, so they recycled that saint to become her second name, Geraldine. Her certificate of baptism added a third name, Patricia, after St. Patrick of Ireland and also her father's middle name; thus, she had two patron saints. Geraldine means "rules by the spear", and although her parents didn't know it at the time, it truly fit. Sheila's fighting spirit became more and more evident over the years.

Sheila never knew her Irish grandparents, and had little contact with her English grandfather Richard Hollick. When he thawed a bit over his daughter's marriage to an Irishman and her adoption of Catholicism, he occasionally used to visit their cramped house on Richmond Street. He would always arrive very stern and pompous, stiff and unsmiling behind his thick moustache, but he usually had some candies for the children.

"Has everyone been good?" he would ask, pulling a bag of sweets from his coat pocket. Sheila, as one of the youngest, waited in great anticipation of the treat, sitting on the stairs, her thin arms hugging her knees to her chest as she shyly looked down at the scene unfolding below her.

Some older brother or sister inevitably piped up with reports about someone else's misbehavior, generally someone younger who couldn't defend themselves. "Sheila left the door open and the dog came in and made a mess," one of her brothers volunteered. The hope was that the small share of goodies would spread farther if they incriminated a few of the younger children. "Well then, there will be no treats for her," her grandfather replied, a judge pronouncing sentence. Sheila slunk back up the stairs to her bed, curled into a ball, and cried. For a child who rarely saw candy and lived in poverty, this proved quite traumatic and cruel. While the relationship between Nellie and her father thawed over the years, and some of Sheila's older siblings visited his home and received assistance with school costs, Sheila came to feel no affection for him. Richard Hollick died in 1930 when she was eleven years old, and left his entire estate to his son Gilbert.

William and Nellie O'Carroll lived in their tiny Richmond Street house through WW1, the Depression, and the Second World War. They raised ten children there, and even built a bomb shelter in the back garden in the 1940s. 122 Richmond Street remained the O'Carroll home until Sheila's parents died in the early 1950s. They always paid their rent on time, but never owned it.

Their home was crowded not just with children, but with laughter and love, despite many hardships and arguments. It provided the window through which Sheila measured the world, and the foundation for the adult she became.

Sheila in the pram with sisters Kathleen (middle) and Nora (left), 1921

The O'Carrolls, circa late 1919.
Standing in the back: William O'Carroll (Sheila's father)
Back Row L-R: Agnes, Bill, Eileen, Bernard, Kevin
Front Row L-R: Patrick, Nora, Kathleen, Sheila held by her mother Nellie
(not yet born Tess 1923)

CHAPTER 3
122 RICHMOND STREET:
1920's

NO IRISH NEED APPLY

The sign was posted in the window of every Coventry machine shop Sheila's father passed. As he kept walking, his despair grew. It didn't matter that he was a skilled worker, the O' in front of his name eliminated him from consideration by the English bosses. After years of struggle, guerilla warfare, and deaths on both sides, Ireland had finally achieved a measure of independence from England in 1919, but strong anti-Irish and anti-Catholic feelings remained. William O'Carroll, like many Irish, had originally come to England to improve his prospects, but now, after WW1, found every door slammed in his face.

When it became clear that it was impossible for him to find any work in Coventry, he went back to Ireland, to the city of Cork, and landed a job at the new Ford factory. Ford needed lots of skilled workers in the machine shop as they switched their assembly line from war-time tractors to the popular Model T car, and William had no trouble getting hired. Living on his own as frugally as possible, he saved every penny he could to send back to Coventry for Nellie and his children.

There had been a lot of violence on both sides during the War of Independence, and Ireland was still a dangerous place to be. Agitation for an Irish Republic had grown after WW1, and Dublin's Kilmainham prison was filled with rebels and their supporters. The British executed the ring-leaders in the prison yard, including the Mayor of Cork. City streets were being patrolled by the ruthless "Black and Tans," the temporary policemen recruited as mercenaries to beef up the ranks of the British controlled Irish Constabulary. They were known for their brutality against the Irish, so for William, just trying to make enough to support his family and survive, it was best to keep his head down, his mouth shut, and stay out of their way.

William O'Carroll was fiercely proud of his Irish Catholic roots and had always supported the goal of an Irish Republic free from England, but he was not in favor of violence to achieve those ends. Instead, he and Nellie worked behind the front lines for the Republican movement and allowed 122 Richmond Street to become a part of an "underground railroad." Irish partisans travelling between Ireland and England, passing along political information or running to avoid arrest, were secretly given a meal or a place to sleep late at night in the O'Carroll home, and were smuggled away early in the morning.

Sheila was not the only child who saw a secret traveller. Her older sister Kathleen also got up late one night after hearing a noise. Creeping partway down the stairs, she saw a man, fully dressed, laying on the floor. Not knowing if he was asleep or dead, she rushed, frightened, back to her bed and hid. When she got up hours later, he was gone. "Mama," she asked Nellie, looking around. "Where is that man? Who was he?"

"What man?" Nellie said, stirring a pot on the stove, her back to Kathleen. "There was no man here."

"There was! I think he was asleep, but he had his boots on!" Kathleen insisted.

Nellie turned around, put both hands on young Kathleen's shoulders, looked at her sternly, and said again, "You didn't see anyone. There was no one here."

Sheila's father stayed in Cork for two or three years, supporting his family as best he could, and returned to Coventry only infrequently when money allowed. Meanwhile, he remained involved on the edges of the political movement and came to know Eamon de Valera, later both the Prime Minister and the President of Ireland. William was a member of the Sinn Fein political party his entire life, and a founder of the Coventry Irish Club. He may have had to live in England, but he was always proudly Irish.

The ten O'Carroll children were spread out over fifteen years, beginning with Agnes and ending with Tess, who was born when William had returned from Cork. Their lives in Coventry were rough and tumble, but fun, despite financial struggles and pervasive anti-Irish sentiments. As the children headed off down Richmond Street each morning for school, they were taunted by the Protestant kids. "Dirty Cat Licks! Dirty Cat Licks!" was shouted at them, and the O'Carroll's shouted back, "Proddy Dogs! Proddy Dogs!" At the end of the street, the Protestants turned one way, and the Catholics the other, sticks and stones and more insults thrown in both directions.

There were also more subtle forms of discrimination. The landlord always came in person to collect the rent, as was the practice at the time. He had the habit of walking into the house without knocking because the O'Carrolls were "just Irish," after all, and Catholic to boot. Nellie, finally fed up with the abuse and disrespect, had a plan and was ready and waiting for him one day. She put a tub of dirty water just inside the door and pretended to be washing the floors as she waited. The landlord came striding down Richmond Street and walked in the front door unannounced as usual. Just at the moment he opened the door, Nellie lifted the tub and threw the dirty water over the threshold, soaking him. "Oh my dear, I am so sorry! I was washing the floor and I never heard you knock!" she said as the landlord stood shocked and sputtering, water running down his suit jacket. "Shall I run to the kitchen and get a rag so you can dry up?" The children hid, giggling, in the scullery. Nellie's message was received loud and clear. Thereafter, the landlord knocked and waited to be admitted.

With all those mouths to feed, the pay packets William sent back from Ireland never stretched far enough. Nellie did the best she could with what she could get, but nutritious food was often not available or not affordable. Potatoes and root vegetables that could be grown in the tiny back garden were important, but not enough. Meat was eaten only a couple of times a week, the roast from Sunday's dinner made to stretch out into several meals. It often became soup with little protein or just the bones to flavor it. Porridge was a staple. "Bubble and Squeak" was made from leftover potatoes fried together with bits of vegetables like cabbage. Milk was rare. Eggs were a treat. Some meals were just bread and jam. Fresh citrus fruit like oranges were a rare treat that the O'Carroll children saw only at Christmas if they were lucky.

Good food was in such short supply that by the age of three, Sheila had rickets, a bone disease caused by malnutrition. Her bones were so weak that her legs couldn't support her. She wasn't getting the dietary nutrients found in milk, eggs, and fish, or enough Vitamin D. Her brothers and sisters weren't either, but Sheila was the youngest and the only one to fall victim to the disease. In the heavily industrial area of the Midlands in the early 1920s, there wasn't enough Vitamin D-rich sunshine getting through the smog, and there certainly wasn't enough good food at 122 Richmond Street.

With William still away in Ireland, Nellie was left to manage the situation on her own. She bundled Sheila into a cart and pulled her to the local doctor to see what could be done. Looking down his nose at the poor "Irish" woman with her large brood of children, he told her, "There's not much we can do except to break the child's legs. We'll reset them and put her in braces so they grow straighter." Nellie was appalled. Not willing to accept such a dire prognosis, she found out what she could about treatments and sought a second opinion. Leaving the other children in the care of their older siblings, she carried Sheila in her arms to the train and took her to a specialist, who correctly diagnosed the source of the problem and gave the order for better food. Already struggling to feed her large family, Nellie felt the weight of the world on her shoulders.

"That egg is for Sheila!" Nellie ordered, as she shooed away the rest of the bunch from the precious commodity she had carefully squirreled away. "Sheila, make sure you drink that milk before the others do." William brought back good Irish cheese and butter when he could. Over time, with careful attention and sacrifices to get the nutritious food she needed to grow, eventually little Sheila could walk and run again.

The rest of the O'Carroll kids did what they could to help out the family's food supply. The older brothers were sent to the local butcher shop to get free scraps and bones for soup. "Could we have some bones please, Sir?" they asked. "For the dog," they added, thinking this would be a better incentive. One day the astute butcher asked, "and what's the name of your dog?' never having seen one with them. The ragtag bunch shuffled and looked awkwardly away. There was no answer because there was no dog, just as the butcher had suspected.

At other times the older boys sneaked over the concrete wall separating 122 Richmond Street from the Stoke Ex-Serviceman's Club on Clay Lane, a private club next door, to raid the apple trees. The club responded by cementing large shards of glass on top of the wall to make it impossible for the O'Carroll boys to climb over without shredding their hands and knees. One time Sheila's older brother Kevin lassoed a tame duck from the same property and proudly brought it home for supper. "Where did you get THAT??" Nellie interrogated him, aghast. "We're not so poor that we have to STEAL!" Kevin was immediately marched back to return it and make amends.

Nellie might have been poor, but she was proud. One day, she was stopped on the street by a neighbour. "What a kind woman you are," said the lady. "Whatever do you mean?" asked Nellie, taken aback and immediately suspicious. This woman had rarely spoken to her and usually looked down her nose at the O'Carrolls. "Why, you have so little and yet you've taken in all those poor children to care for," the nosy neighbor cooed. Nellie knew immediately how this rumour had started. "These are ALL my own children," she replied indignantly, and, head held high, walked on. One of Sheila's older sisters, perhaps dramatic Nora, not wanting to be seen as part of such a large and poor family, had been spreading the story that her mother was taking care of less fortunate children!

It wasn't all hard times, however. Even as children, the O'Carrolls enjoyed a joke and making fun. One of the older boys' chores was to take the family's linens to the local public laundry, the heavy bundle rolled up and put into the baby carriage to push down the street. On more than one occasion as they approached a group of the local women gossiping on the sidewalk, the children grinned at each other, let go of the carriage handle and gave it a little push. It started rolling faster and faster down the hill, with the boys in pursuit yelling, "Save the baby! Save the baby!" As planned, the brothers stopped the carriage just before it rolled into traffic, and then burst into laughter. Even Nellie was amused when she heard about it later. "You are so wicked!" she admonished. "You'd better include that in your next confessions before Mass."

All the O'Carroll children attended the local parochial school and were taught by the nuns, and every one of them was subjected to the strict discipline and occasional cruelty of the Sisters. William and Nellie, staunchly Catholic, were not sympathetic to their children's complaints. More than once, gregarious Sheila came home to report that she was made to kneel for hours on the hard slate hallway floor as punishment for chatting in class. When the Sister wasn't looking, Sheila would sit back on her heels to take the pressure off her knees, but if the Sister caught her she'd smack her with a ruler and make her kneel for even longer. Sheila's brother Bernard came home distraught one day to tell his parents that Father Murphy was angry with him. "I didn't have anything to tell him in confession," he said. "I haven't done anything wrong this week, but he wouldn't believe me! He said I was a liar." Sheila's father grabbed Bernard by the collar and, with some help from Bernard's brother Bill, threw him out of the house onto the street for defying the priest. Outspoken Nora had so many confrontations with the nuns that she had to leave the school and live for a time with her Grandfather Hollick. The rigidity of the church in those days turned Nora and Bernard off religion for the rest of their lives.

Through the 1920s and 30s, William O'Carroll made sure to take as many of his children as he could, one by one, back to visit their roots in Ireland. When it was finally Sheila's turn, she was desperately seasick crossing the Irish Channel, but recovered by the time they got to Abbeyleix and went on to Blarney Castle. It was a tradition for William to take each of his children to kiss the ancient Blarney Stone. He steadied Sheila as she lay on the hard wall and tipped her head backwards to kiss the old rock, ensuring, as the myth goes, that she would have the gift of the gab for the rest of her life. It worked.

What William and Nellie couldn't give their children in possessions they made up for in imagination. William entranced the youngest children with his tales of "the little people", the leprechauns, back in Ireland. The belief in the "fairies at the bottom of the garden" also filled their dreams with pleasant images. For years, Sheila's father was one of the organizers of the Workingman's Parade in Coventry, dressing as a pirate and thrilling his children. It didn't have to cost him a lot to have fun.

In 1924, when Sheila was just five, the oldest of her sisters, eighteen-year-old Agnes, left home. She joined her Irish aunts (William's sisters) in New York City and went on to nursing school. Not long after that, Nora emigrated as well, and went to business school, and in 1930 Kathleen joined them and became a nurse too. By the time she was eleven, three of Sheila's older sisters were gone and her only contact with them was through letters. She no longer had to share her bed with two others, but she missed them. From her perspective as a child, they were living glamourous, exciting lives far away in America.

On October 27th, 1932, thirteen-year-old Sheila sent a cheery note across the ocean to her big sister Agnes, updating her on the ordinary things happening at home.

"I expect you'll be rather busy, but I'm sure you'd like to hear from me as it's quite a long while since I last wrote."

The big news item was that their parents William and Nellie had gone to play whist at a sausage supper on Guy Fawkes' night and won a prize.

Do you go to whist drives or do you like dancing better? Sheila asked.

"Kev and Bill are interested in dancing, but Bernard is more interested in his operating. He's a film operator at the Brown Theatre, don't you know? The Brown's been done up and changed into a spiffing place now and we would like to see him gradually rise to manager, wouldn't that be great?"

"Hoping you have enough ice and snow to skate on and Happy wishes for a Jolly Xmas. I remain your affectionate sister Sheila XXXXX"

Sheila's mother Nellie felt the same fascination for life beyond Coventry. She had always wanted to travel the world and once, without consulting William, she took the funds he had carefully squirreled away for a trip back to Ireland and on a whim purchased tickets for Spain and France instead. William quickly cashed them in. Nellie finally achieved her dream of seeing America and her daughter Nora, whom she had not seen for eighteen years, only months before she died. But in the earlier days of financial strain, the furthest she got was to the train station in Coventry. She liked to buy a penny ticket for the platform and sit quietly, removed for a bit of time from the reality of her life, watching other more fortunate people come and go on their travels.

Despite the hardships, every one of Sheila's siblings finished school and went on to careers and productive lives lived around the world. They became skilled tradespeople and professionals. Nora and Eileen had senior administrative positions. Kevin, Bill, and Bernard started their own successful machine engineering business in Coventry before Kevin joined the Merchant Navy and moved to the USA. Bill served in the Merchant Navy as well. Patrick left his job in the USA for Canada when WW2 started and became an air gunner in the Canadian Air Force. After the war, he worked in the oil fields in the Middle East, and then came home to England and married the girl who had lived across the street from 122 Richmond Street. Agnes had a full career in the US Medical Corps, retiring with the rank of major, after serving in Korea and Germany. Kathleen was a WW2 nurse as well, a lieutenant who served on the front lines in the Pacific. Even Sheila's younger sister Tess joined the British Air Force in 1941 as soon as she was old enough, and in her later years became a teacher.

All the O'Carroll clan lived their lives with humour, optimism, and great love for each other despite their distance. They shared their adventures and views of the world in prolific letters. Sadly, one by one, half of Sheila's siblings died from cancer in their 50s and 60s. But despite challenges and illnesses and disappointments, they refused to whine, choosing instead to meet adversity head on. It was an O'Carroll trait that Sheila shared.

Shoulders back, chin up, and jolly well carry on.

October 1926
Back row left to right: Kathleen, Nora, Kevin, Bill
Front row left to right: Patrick, Tess on mother Nellie's knee, Bernard, Sheila
(age seven)
Missing: Agnes, Eileen, father William

Sheila, 1936, Cycling Club

Sheila's father, William Patrick O'Carroll (1873 to 1953)
Picture circa 1950

Sheila's mother, Nellie (Hollick) O'Carroll 1882 to 1954
Picture circa late 1930s

CHAPTER 4
W/22123:
1939 TO 1945

August 25ᵗʰ, 1939 started as a typical summer day in Coventry until someone left an ordinary-looking bicycle leaning against a lamppost not far from the O'Carroll home on Richmond Street. There were lots of bicycles parked everywhere, so unfortunately no one paid any attention to this one. It contained a bomb from the Irish Republican Army, the IRA, and when it exploded later that day, five people were killed and another seventy were injured. Sheila's father William was heartbroken and appalled. This terrorist fringe was not the Republican movement he had supported for so many years, and as he expected, the citizens of Coventry and the rest of the country again turned against the Irish after years of relative calm.

Then, just a few days later, the public's attention was deflected by a much bigger threat. On September 3ʳᵈ, Britain declared war on Germany, and the Second World War was set in motion. It wasn't a surprise to anyone who had been following the build up of Nazi power in the late 1930s, and the average British citizen expected it to be a short and successful confrontation. What great excitement! *We beat the Germans once before and we can beat them again! Rule Britannia!*

In that late summer of 1939, Sheila was twenty years old, and her life was about to change dramatically.

By then, she had been living in Bournemouth on the south coast of England for about a year, sharing a room in a boarding house with her best friend Mary Greenaway. Sheila and Mary were classmates at Stoke Park Secondary School for Girls in Coventry, and despite their social differences became close friends. Mary came from a small middle class Protestant family, unlike Sheila's large Catholic clan, and was comfortably well-off. Her parents could afford the tuition fee for secondary school. Sheila, on the other hand, couldn't have attended Stoke Park without the benefit of a scholarship, but, thankfully, she had always been a good student in both math and English and easily won the financial aid she needed. In those days in England, students left school at fourteen and moved on to a factory or a job in a shop. Attending secondary school meant training for better jobs in banks and offices, or going even further to university.

"Ohhh, jolly good, Sheila's won a place in secondary school!" teased her older brothers. "It's not just any school, don't you know!" Sheila replied with a laugh in her best put-on plummy English accent and with her nose in the air. "I'm attending Stoke Park Secondary School *for refined young ladies.* The brothers guffawed. "Refined indeed," Bernard laughed, "you little snob!" as he poked her in the ribs.

Those were happy teenage years for Sheila. She studied hard and did well academically. She played field hockey and didn't miss the knuckle-rapping nuns from her elementary school days. Without a care in the world, she was looking forward to a bright future even as war loomed over Europe.

In 1938, Sheila and Mary both got jobs with Barclay's Bank in Bournemouth and put into place a plan to move out of Coventry. Leaving home for the first time, they headed to a new city and, they hoped, some adventures away from the eyes of their parents. It was near the end of the

Depression and neither of them had any money for travelling, so they concocted a plan to ride their bicycles together the 150 miles or so south to Bournemouth. When Mary's doting father learned of this risky idea, he put this foot down and purchased a train ticket for her instead, and Mary, always less adventurous than Sheila, gladly accepted it. Sheila knew that her own father would not approve of her riding all that distance alone, but not wanting to ask him for the train fare, she made up a story. "There's been a bit of a change of plans," she told her parents as she was tying her suitcase on her bicycle on the morning of her departure. "I'm meeting Mary at her house and we'll start off from there. Mary's mother has packed us a big box of food and we might as well load it up at her house." It was a lie, and she hoped her father wouldn't figure it out before she was gone. Sheila made the trip by herself, hitching rides when she could put her bicycle in the back of a truck, and resting in whatever places she could find. If she even considered the risks in the first place, she dismissed them for the potential for adventure. Much like her mother Nellie a generation earlier, Sheila's bicycle was a tool for her independence. She wasn't daunted by the idea of doing something on her own when the circumstances required it.

It turned out that Sheila's and Mary's jobs in the bank were boring, but away from the constraints of parents and with the independence of finally having their own paycheques, life was otherwise fun. Sheila, pretty and round-faced, enjoyed her late teenage years in Bournemouth, meeting new friends and, for the first time in her life, spending carefree days at the beach. Once, riding on the back of a boyfriend's motorbike with the sea salt and wind in her eyes, she contracted a brutal eye infection. The local doctor's only treatment was to cut off her eyelashes so her eyes could drain and heal. They never grew back fully and all her life she lamented the full thick black lashes she left behind in Bournemouth.

On September 3rd, 1939 Sheila was listening to the little radio in their boarding house when the music was interrupted to announce the news that war had been declared. "Mary, Mary, we're at war with Germany!" she screamed. The newspapers were full of blaring headlines that encouraged citizens to sign up and fight for Britain. "We've got to do our part! This is exciting and who knows what we might end up doing! Are you coming with me?" Mary, as usual, declined.

Sheila found the nearest army recruiting station the next day and signed up without her friend Mary and without any discussion with her parents. She became W/22123 of the Auxiliary Territorial Service. The ATS had been formed during WW1 when it was recognized that women were needed to take over non-combatant roles to free up men for front line duties. It was originally called the Women's Army Auxiliary Corps (WAAC), but the name changed to ATS in 1938, and changed again after the war to the Women's Royal Army Corps in February 1949. Young Princess Elizabeth, later to be the Queen, followed Sheila into the ATS near the end of the war and held the same job in the Transport Corps.

It was an exciting time to be a twenty-year-old woman heading into a previously undreamed of adventure. Sheila naïvely thought war sounded like fun. Bright, eager, and enthusiastic to support her country, Sheila's first challenge was going to be telling her Irish father, the man who had taken risks to oppose the British government many times in his life, that she had joined the English army. It had only been a couple of weeks since the bicycle bomb in Coventry, and feelings were still running high. She packed up her few belongings from the boarding house in Bournemouth and went to her parents' home in Coventry before reporting for duty.

"Dad," she said nervously as she set her suitcase inside the front door, "I've got something to tell you. I've joined the army." She waited for his reaction, expecting anger and, worse yet, disappointment in her.

"Ah, Sheila my darlin'," he said in his Irish brogue, with a twinkle in his eyes, "come over here and sit beside me." He put his hand on her arm. "Don't ye know that some of the best generals in the English army have been Irish? I'm proud of ye for doing such a thing." William Patrick O'Carroll was a man who had stood up for the things he believed in, and he expected to see his children do the same.

Sheila reported for duty on September 17th, 1939, exactly two weeks after the declaration of war.

Mary Greenaway never did enlist. Her goals were far less ambitious than Sheila's. She married her boyfriend Wally and they lived all the rest of their lives in Bournemouth. In September 1939, the two school friends chose divergent paths to much different lives, although they couldn't have known that at the time. They stayed in touch for most of the next forty years, but had less and less in common as time passed.

Sheila's first military job turned out to be nothing quite as thrilling as she had anticipated. After basic training and mastering the marching drills, the care and presentation of her uniforms, and all the rules, she was assigned to be a pay clerk, likely based on her experience in a bank. She was good with numbers, but she had hoped for something considerably more important and exciting, and maybe even dangerous, nothing as ordinary as clerical work. What she didn't realize was that many of the skills she learned in basic training would stay with her for the rest of her life. She always efficiently ironed the crispest shirts, starting with collar and moving on to the yoke, the sleeves, and finally the front and back. Perfect pant creases were made by aligning the inside seams. When she sewed on a button, it would never fall off again, and she polished a pair of shoes until you could see your reflection in them. Sheila's beds were made with military precision and perfect hospital corners, with the blankets tight enough to bounce a coin off the mattress. She learned to march when she walked, a habit that persisted into her later years.

Pay parade, the process of formally lining up to receive her army stipend, was a routine so drilled into Sheila that it remained something she would perform on request for decades after the war. When her name was shouted out, "O'CARROLL!", she would march forward, head up, shoulders back. She made a quick halt, smartly slammed her foot down and stood at attention with her arms stiffly at her sides, and then snapped a salute while barking out "O'CARROLL W/22123." When her pay package was held out, she grasped it in her right hand and, in one movement, returned her arms tightly to her sides again, turned sharply on one heel, and crisply marched away. The disciplined posture and serious presentation remained her entire life. Sheila never slouched.

She loved the rules, the structure, and as much as anything, the reliability of the military. She enjoyed the freedom of not worrying about the mundane daily details of life. Someone else arranged where she'd sleep and what she'd eat.

For the next three years, until May of 1942, Sheila was posted to various locations in England and Wales, keeping her rank as a private and sharing her life with other young women in the ATS as the war rolled along. They were from all walks of life and all parts of Britain, and while there were dangers and restrictions, as there were for ordinary citizens, the ATS women enjoyed the sense of adventure and camaraderie the army provided. The military had taken over big private houses as well as convents and schools for billets, and the women were often housed in unheated, drafty dormitories. Sheila was used to sharing her living space, first with her sisters and then with her friend Mary. She had never had a bedroom to herself and didn't expect luxury or privacy. She went to bed with a hot water bottle for comfort and learned the trick of pulling her clothes into her warm bed in the morning to get dressed under the covers before putting her feet on the icy floor.

Even though they experienced minor hardships, Sheila and her ATS friends were removed from many of the everyday struggles of the British people. Despite rationing rules for the general population, there was always enough food in the army. It was a very pleasant change from the shortages of Sheila's life up to that time.

Almost everything was rationed for civilians. A large percentage of Britain's food supply was imported, and the Germans knew that one way to starve out the enemy was to disrupt shipping and limit supplies for both the military and the general population. By 1942, the food for Sheila's family in Coventry was solely dependent on what was allowed in their ration books, plus a few vegetables, particularly potatoes, and any fruit they could find from farmers or grow in their little Victory garden. Their economic situation had improved a bit before the war, but now they were scrimping again like everyone else. Each person got only one fresh egg per week, plus some powdered eggs. They had two ounces of butter and cheese, three pints of milk, eight ounces of sugar, and two ounces of tea. Their weekly meat ration was four ounces of bacon or ham and about one pound of other meat, bones included. Petrol, other fuel, and even clothes were rationed so the needs of the huge military operation could be met first. The O'Carrolls were used to making do, but they struggled and sacrificed like everyone else.

In November of 1940, when Sheila had been in the ATS for little more than a year, her home city of Coventry was brutally bombed by the Nazis. Coventry had become a significant industrial center for war production and its bombing was a strategic hit. The beautiful medieval core of the city, including the 11th century cathedral, was flattened. It was terribly demoralizing for Coventry's citizens to see their lovely city destroyed and innocent civilians killed. The rest of the country was already reeling from the Nazi bombs in other cities. On moonlit nights, the people in Coventry could see the airplanes coming in wave and after wave as the air raid sirens screamed. Amazingly, although the O'Carroll's Richmond Street house was only a short distance from the cathedral, it wasn't hit. The entire street was somehow spared. Sheila's parents William and Nellie, along with her younger sister Tess, survived the bombings in their Anderson shelter in the back yard. As they huddled together, William tracked the sounds of the falling bombs with an ongoing commentary. "Aye, that one was close!" he'd say as the bombs exploded around them. "I think that one's landed on Clay Lane! The next one will be us." Nellie and Tess sat with their hands over the ears and shrieked at each big boom. "Stop it William!" Nellie cried. "Your jokes don't help."

Tess rocked back and forth, shaking and trembling as Nellie tried to comfort her. When it was over, Tess was so terrified of staying in Coventry that she ran away, riding her bicycle and hitching rides to join Sheila at her barracks miles away, the only place she thought she might be safe.

It was sheer luck that all of the O'Carroll family was unscathed, at least physically. Stationed safely away in Nottingham, Sheila listened to the radio reports about Coventry's bombing and was sick with worry until Tess unexpectedly arrived and told her the family had survived. Sheila immediately sent a telegram to her parents to let them know Tess was there, and hoped it would get through despite the destruction and confusion. It was not until three months later, in February 1941, that she was granted a few days leave to go home to visit her family. Coincidentally, it was her twenty-second birthday.

She got off the train and walked to 122 Richmond Street, past the flattened cinema where her brother Bernard used to work, its marquee still standing and ironically announcing the movie "Gone with the Wind". Amidst the rubble from the bombing, Sheila's home was still there housing William and Nellie. "Happy birthday, me darlin'," her father greeted her, wrapping her in a big hug. Nellie wiped the tears from her eyes. "We're so glad to see you," she said, "and that you're safe." "I was worried sick too," Sheila admitted, "and I'm so happy to see you're both okay." She stayed with them only a few days and then had to return to her post.

In May 1942 Sheila was posted to Belfast. There was still a lot of resentment for the English among the Catholic minority in Northern Ireland for their decision many years earlier to split the country and keep the northern counties for themselves. The IRA was continuing to engage in small acts of guerrilla violence against the English in an effort to make clear their message that the English must leave. All military personnel were ordered to remain on the base at all times, as rumours were rampant that the IRA supporters would grab anyone in a British uniform to tar and feather them, regardless of gender. Their objective was not only to injure and humiliate the individual victim, but also to undermine British authority. The terrorists wouldn't know that Sheila was Catholic with an O' in her name, and her own Irish father had supported the Republican movement his entire life. To them, she was now nothing more than a target in the wrong uniform, perhaps even a traitor to her Irish roots. For the next eight months while she remained in Northern Ireland, Sheila avoided all trouble.

What Sheila really wanted to do was to get to the action in Europe and see some excitement beyond her pay ledgers. The war was dragging along and she knew she hadn't signed up to be just a clerk. Finally, in February of 1943, she was accepted into the Transport Corps training program as a driver/mechanic, and by June of that year her dreams of adventure were about to become reality. At last she was about to step into a very important job.

The women drivers of the Transport Corps were crucial cogs in a very big wheel. They were relied on to keep the army moving, being responsible to maintain, repair, and drive a variety of different military vehicles. Often it was big unwieldy lorries, weighing up to three tons, that they collected from the manufacturers, delivered to army depots for outfitting and deployment, and drove in convoys long distances to military units or to the ports for overseas shipment.

Sheila's job of driver/mechanic required stamina, physical strength, and good driving skills to handle the big beasts. There was no such thing as power steering or even signal lights, the clutch was stiff, and the gears were often uncooperative. The trucks were loud, cold, and uncomfortable, but the women in the Transport Corps had to keep them moving and on time and see them to the right locations. It was a challenging and exciting responsibility.

Sheila had grown up listening to her father and her mechanic brothers talking about engines. She was used to greasy motor parts spread out on the kitchen table as they rebuilt their motor bikes or other machines. The gritty business end of changing oil and spark plugs and fixing tires didn't intimidate her. She welcomed it. Her wardrobe was often a pair of dirty coveralls and boots and a scarf tied around her head to keep her hair out of the grease. It was not a glamorous job and her fingernails were often dirty. The hours were long, but Sheila grew to love it, waking up early in the cold dark before dawn to start the lorries and get moving. She knew the outcome of the war depended on it.

The women of the Transport Corps were trained to drive anything, from staff cars to big lorries and ambulances, and even motorcycles to deliver messages, but unless they could competently read a map and decipher instructions, their driving skills were useless. In wartime, signposts were often removed or changed to confuse the enemy, so navigating was a significant challenge, especially if they were driving on secondary roads on dark overnight trips with lights off for the blackouts. Getting lost would have been a dangerous mistake, so the drivers followed each other carefully and closely in a convoy. Their big yellow leather gauntlets, reaching almost to the elbow, were the only indicators they had to signal a turn, their arms thrust out the open window in the cold air. Their leather jerkins, hip length and tan colored, were worn over their uniforms as an extra layer to keep out the cold in the unheated trucks.

Sheila's army boots were eventually passed down to her sons and were still in use long after the war until they could no longer be repaired. She kept her driver's wardrobe pieces for years. She had been proud to wear them and they remained a tangible link to an important time in her life.

Coventry, September 1940
Sheila with her parents

February 1940, Winchester Hampshire England
Sheila age twenty-one

Sheila, July 1940

Sheila O'Carroll, W/22123

CHAPTER 5
THE WAR YEARS END:
1945

It was D-Day, June 1944 when Sheila, now a corporal, finally felt like she was doing something important to help the war effort. She had a year of experience driving big lorries and as a motorcycle driver was zipping messages and dispatches between military bases. As an ATS driver, she had helped to move the thousands of troops and the myriad supplies in preparation for the D-Day invasion. Things had not been going well for the Allies up to that point, and the Nazis had overrun France, Poland, the Netherlands, and Belgium. By the summer of 1944, as the Allies moved into Belgium and Holland and it began to look like they had a chance to win the war, Sheila was at last posted to the European side of the English Channel, and was excited to think she would finally see some real action and have some adventures on the Continent.

She didn't expect it to change her life forever.

The suffering of Europe's citizens under Nazi occupation got worse and worse during the last years of the war, as the supplies of food and other necessities steadily dwindled to almost nothing. In the widespread famine of 1944/45 in the Netherlands, even the country's famous tulip bulbs became a source of food. Although the liberation of the Netherlands and Belgium by the 1ˢᵗ Canadian Army was underway at the time, food supplies had not caught up, and Sheila witnessed first hand the devastating hunger of the ordinary local citizens.

Travelling in a convoy of lorries through the Belgium countryside, Sheila and the other drivers stopped at mid-day to have a stretch and eat their packed lunches on the side of the road. There was more food than they could eat or had time to enjoy, so when they were finished, they tossed the leftovers into the ditch: bread crusts, bits of apples, a few pieces of cheese, and a boiled egg. There'd be more food at tea when they got to their destination. They'd been instructed not to waste, but the leftover lunches would be inedible after a day in their hot trucks. Instead of bringing them back to the barracks just to be thrown in the garbage, they thought by leaving the bits and pieces on the roadside some small animals or a farm dog might benefit. They climbed back into the big lorries, started them up, and slowly pulled away to continue the journey. As Sheila looked out her rear view mirror to make sure the rest of the convoy was with her, what she saw shocked her. Emaciated old men and women with ragged children were scrambling up from the embankments and hedges to grab the discarded food. They had been watching the convoy and waiting. The leftovers were not going to go to the dogs.

That scene left a lasting impression on Sheila. She was appalled by what she had witnessed, and felt a little guilty about how much she enjoyed being well fed in the army. The indelible memory of those hungry people came back to her years later when she had her own children, and it made her sad. By then she could identify with the worry and pain of those parents struggling to feed their children.

By the last months of the war, Sheila was driving large military ambulances, the same big lorries she was used to but outfitted to carry people instead of cargo and to transport survivors freed from the concentration camps. She wasn't a medic and her responsibility was just to drive without any physical contact with her passengers, but she always watched as they were loaded and unloaded from the back of her ambulance. Many were just walking skeletons, others needing help to move and were barely human looking, wearing a few filthy rags for clothes.

While horrified by the condition of her passengers, at that time Sheila didn't know the terrible things they had experienced and survived. No one knew or could imagine the extent of the horrific concentration camps until the facts became public after the war. Much later in her life when she was asked about it, she described her feeling this way: "*We had no idea what had been done to those people. And maybe that was better so we could just do our jobs. But I'm ashamed of how I reacted with such disgust for the poor victims.*"

The survivors Sheila transported likely came from the Bergen-Belsen camp in Northern Germany. That was where Anne Frank died in March 1945, only a few weeks before it was liberated by the British army. They found 60,000 starving and ill people suffering from typhus and dysentery in the camp with no food, water, or basic sanitation, and the British military ambulances that Sheila drove were used to move them out. The impact of seeing those emaciated and suffering people never left her. For the rest of her life she could not tolerate injustice or bigotry or cruelty.

At the time, though, Sheila was able to push those scenes to the back of her mind, as did the other women she served with. They were young and carefree, and most of their experiences in the last year of the war in Europe were happy ones. Sheila loved her life in the military and she focused on having fun.

On a warm February day in 1945, just before her twenty-sixth birthday, Sheila was leading a convoy of trucks in Belgium and arrived at an intersection where a Canadian military policeman was directing traffic. The road signs had been removed as usual and she wasn't sure of her directions to the next town, so she signaled for the convoy to stop and got out to ask the MP for help. "The main road's closed so it's pretty complicated," he told her, "but I'm off duty in ten minutes and I'll take you there. Just follow my jeep." Sheila walked back to tell the rest of her drivers what was going on. "Turn off your engines and relax," she said. "We're going to wait for an escort from that Canadian MP." She rested her chin on her folded arms on the open window of her truck while she watched him moving the military traffic, and whispered quietly to herself, "*Now there's a man I'd like to get to know.*"

Sheila, like all the other women in the military, had met lots of soldiers, sailors, and airmen over the last five years of the war. Women were outnumbered by men. For a short time in Ireland, she had a boyfriend named Barney. There were dances and dates with Americans, but she found them too confident and brash, and occasionally with Australians, but she couldn't stand their attitude to women, insulting her good Irish name when they called every girl a Sheila. She wasn't looking for a serious romance yet, and no one had really struck a lasting spark with her. Somehow, though, this Canadian made her feel different that the others had.

Tall and good looking, the traffic-directing provost was a farmer from Ontario, far from home and very lonely. Sheila was an outgoing, fun-loving, adventurous woman. Opposites attracted, and at a crossroads in Belgium, a relationship began which lasted for the next forty-five years.

That quiet Canadian soldier was William John Brown Eccles, the oldest son of ten children born and raised on a farm in Mount Forest. It was a long name for a humble man, but he was known as Brownie, from his mother's maiden name. Prior to the war, he had only ever worked with his father on the farm, and it was his sole ambition to continue to do just that for the rest of his life. When Sheila was enjoying her classes at Stoke Park Secondary School on the other side of the Atlantic Ocean, Brownie couldn't wait to finish grade eight at his local one-room school so he could get to work on the farm. His grammar was imperfect and his spelling was bad, but he was intelligent, gentle, and kind, the quieter one in a family of outgoing, fun-loving siblings. The Eccles all loved music and step-dancing, and just prior to the war had won many competitions at the Canadian National Exhibition in Toronto as a family square dancing team. Brownie had never pictured his life as including a war in Europe.

Brownie had reluctantly enlisted in the fall of 1941 after receiving his selection papers. Arriving at the designated regiment in London, Ontario, he found a recruitment set-up with several tables for various branches and units, and other recruits like him lined up at each. He didn't know where he should go or what he wanted to do, so he headed to the only table with no one waiting. It turned out to be the military police. *At least,* he thought, *it might be safer than the infantry.* He was wrong.

Military life was not his chosen vocation and he hoped it would end quickly. On his last pass home to the family farm after finishing his basic training, just before he was shipped out to England, Brownie overstayed his leave and was late reporting back to his unit. He would have preferred to just stay home and forget the whole thing. He was arrested by a fellow MP and as punishment for being Absent Without Leave (AWL), even briefly, spent most of the voyage in the ship's kitchen, peeling mountains of potatoes.

With the 1st Canadian Infantry Division, Brownie spent his first months overseas stationed in England, policing the Canadian soldiers waiting to be sent off to fight in Europe, and training, training, training. He was bored and wondered why he was there. Then, finally, in July 1943, almost eighteen months after he had enlisted, he saw his first view of the action in the invasion of Sicily, and after that the invasion of mainland Italy.

"Oh, do tell me all about Italy!" Sheila coaxed soon after they had met. "It sounds so lovely and exotic. I've always wanted to travel there."

Brownie was a reluctant storyteller, but he shared a couple of his experiences. He needed to tell someone about the things that had happened to him, and he had trouble putting in writing how he felt in his letters back home.

" My troop ship was torpedoed in the Mediterranean on the way to Sicily," he told Sheila. "Because I'm an MP, it was my job to make sure all the troops abandoned the ship in an orderly way, and then when they were all off, I could jump overboard too. Problem was, I don't know how to swim very well. I didn't grow up anywhere near a beach or a pool. I had a lifejacket and I just hoped it would hold me up in the water and I could paddle well enough to get to the shore or be rescued." He laughed. "I took the time to take my boots off, which we weren't supposed to do, but I knew I couldn't swim with those dragging me down. I tied them together and slung them around my neck before jumping in the water."

"Go on then," Sheila encouraged him. "What happened next?"

"Well, I didn't drown," he joked. "I made it to land holding onto a piece of debris with some of my men, and then we hid in an orange grove until we could reconnect with our company. The surprising part is that one of the men who helped pull us into shore was my cousin Arthur. I didn't even know he was there!"

"That's so exciting!" Sheila enthused.

"Not really," he shrugged. "It was too hot and I got sick of eating oranges."

Months later, still in Italy, Brownie was on another ship carrying a load of prisoners of war, assigned as one of the Provosts to supervise their transport, when this ship too was struck by a torpedo. The ship's captain quickly determined there was a small chance he could save the ship and his crew and get safely to the nearby shore if he went full speed ahead, staying on top of the water to keep his damaged boat from sinking. Unfortunately, there was no time to get all the POWs up onto the deck without risking, or sacrificing, the lives of the Canadian soldiers on board, and so it meant some prisoners below the water line were washed out or drowned. Brownie and the other Canadian MPs could only stand by helplessly, unable to save them. It was a long time before he shared that story with Sheila. It bothered him deeply that ordinary soldiers, some of them likely farmers just like him who didn't want to be at war, had had to die so cruelly.

Being a military policeman was not safer than being in the artillery as Brownie had originally hoped, and Italy in particular turned out to be very dangerous for him. "I was patrolling a street in a little town just days after the Allies had captured it," Brownie recounted to Sheila, "and we were fired on by a sniper. I was with two other MP's, one walking on my right side and one on my left. The first shot hit the man on the right in his arm, knocking him to the ground. A split second later the next shot hit the man on my left in the chest, also dropping him. I couldn't see where the shots were coming from and I figured I'd be next, so I dove for the street. I wasn't hit but I lay there in the dirt and didn't move, pretending to be shot and hoping the sniper believed me. I stayed there until the rest of the unit was able to move in and neutralize the shooter."

"What happened to the other two?" Sheila asked, spellbound.

"Oh, they were okay. No one died," Brownie told her, looking away. She didn't know if she should believe him.

By the time Sheila met Brownie in Belgium after his near-death experiences in Italy, he was sick of the war. He wanted nothing more than to go home. He missed the closeness of his family and the peace and productivity of the farm, and wanted his hands in the dirt growing things, not destroying them. In his years since arriving in Europe, Brownie had not had any romantic interests, but was still writing occasional letters to a girl in Mount Forest he had been seeing before he left. He was lonely, and the chance encounter with this pretty, plucky English girl was just what he needed to cheer him up. He was smitten.

One of the advantages of being a military policeman was easy access to a vehicle without the restrictions of wartime gasoline rationing. When Brownie met Sheila in the spring of 1945, his jeep provided the opportunity and freedom to woo her. They took lots of pictures to send home, laughing with their friends, arms around each other, leaning on his jeep. *"After the party,"* Sheila scrawled on the back of one picture showing them cuddled together on a pile of hay in a field. Those fun years were the equivalent of the college days of later generations. The difference was that they had no graduation date, and didn't know what might come next or when the war would end. They were making the most of the good times and the friendships they found with civilians as well as army buddies.

Some of their friends were young Belgian women who fell in love with Canadian soldiers stationed with Brownie, others were ordinary folks working in the local businesses who were happy to do what they could for the Allies who had rescued them from Nazi occupation. One of Sheila and Brownie's closest friends was an older woman in Ghent who owned a café on Butter Market Street. Something about the wartime love affair between the cheery English girl and the gentle Canadian farmer appealed to her sense of romance. Even though she spoke little English, and Sheila spoke only a little French, she took them under her wing and many of their snatched times together in Ghent were spent in a little bed and breakfast room above her café. In the café owner's letters and cards over the next many years, she always signed off as "votre Mamma de Ghent."

On August 1ˢᵗ, 1945, Sheila and Brownie were married in a civil ceremony at City Hall in Ghent. It was just across the street from "Mamma's" café, where they went afterward to celebrate. They wore their military uniforms as required, but Sheila carried a small bouquet of flowers, the only breach of the rule about adorning her uniform. Their marriage "certificate" was a little book in two languages, French and Flemish. It incorrectly listed Brownie's year of birth as 1920. It wasn't until he got home to Canada that his mother corrected him. "You were born in 1919!" she said, shaking her head at his mistake. He had always thought he was a whole year younger. Proud as she was to be an Irish Catholic, Sheila abandoned her religion to become a Protestant like her husband, although he hadn't asked her to do that. It was a decision she regretted in the years to come.

For Brownie, Sheila also gave up the opportunity to visit Paris on a weekend leave. It was only a short train ride from Ghent and she was dying to see it, but Brownie, never the traveller and sick of Europe, didn't want to go. "Why would I want to see another old city?" he asked her. He was happy to spend his valuable free time with Sheila and not waste it on sight seeing. With regret, she acquiesced.

"I didn't go to Paris (the City of Love) because I was *in* love," she said bitterly years later. "I should have just gone by myself."

Sheila and Brownie were granted a couple of weeks of special leave to spend their honeymoon at the Blankenburge Beach on the north coast of Belgium. Unfortunately, their time together was cut short when Sheila got a painful kidney infection and ended up in the local hospital. Brownie had no option but to leave her there and return to his posting, married but alone, in love but lonely.

He was never a great communicator, especially when it involved emotions, but Brownie wrote to his sister Evelyn about a month after the wedding.

What do Mother and Dad think of me getting married to an English girl? I hope that they don't mind, but I guess it doesn't make much difference if they do mind, for she's my wife, not anyone else's. I just hope that you will all like her half as much as I do for I think that there is no one better.

The young woman he was writing to back in Mount Forest throughout the war was under the impression that Brownie was promised to her. In his lonely letters he hadn't done anything to change that until he met Sheila. After the wedding, he wrote to his own mother to ask her to pass along the news for him. He didn't know how to tell her.

As soon as their honeymoon was over, Sheila and Brownie had to go back to their respective postings. Although peace had been declared a few months earlier, they were still on active duty. There was still a lot of work for the military to do before they could discharge their personnel. They met when they could find small chunks of time and received permission, if the distances were not too far and the travel possible. In reality, they spent little time together over the next six months, and Brownie's letters to Sheila reflected the loneliness he felt away from her. Their leaves together were a fleeting luxury, bits of time snatched to be a married couple.

With the war ended, thousands of troops were de-mobilized. The ATS was no longer required at the same strength, so Sheila's army days were terminated. Besides, as a married woman, she no longer qualified to be in the military. Governments were broke and couldn't afford to keep the large armies they hoped they no longer needed. In September 1945, mere weeks after her wedding, she was sent back to Coventry to live with her parents at 122 Richmond Street. There was nowhere else for Sheila to go while she waited for instructions to travel to Canada with her new husband.

Sheila was officially discharged on October 7th, 1945. She pulled the government envelope out of the mailbox at her parents' home, tore it open and read her unit commander's final assessment of her service, and smiled. *"Hard-working, efficient, and reliable. Has shown great enthusiasm for her work. Has a good manner, is trustworthy and sensible, and has a pleasant disposition."* It turned out to be an accurate forecast of her character for the rest of her life.

Sheila had loved her years in the military and was sorry to leave it behind, but that part of her life was now over forever. She was a married woman, a war bride (a term she hated), and was waiting for her turn to be sent to

Canada. And within a very short time, she learned she was also going to be a mother.

Sheila (bottom centre) with other ATS drivers, circa 1945

Dirty work, circa 1944

Sheila, ready for a convoy, 1945

Sheila's ambulance on the Culemborg Ferry, 1945

Destelbergen Chateau, near Ghent, Belgium. "C" PLN, 753 Coy, RASC

```
                                                   S E C R E T

                    HOSPITAL  LOCATION  LIST

                 On the route CAMBRAI to AREA D.
            Cases may be sent to any of these Hospitals.

  96 (Br) Gen Hosp    KAIN, Nr. TOURNAI                       H9235

 113 (Br) Gen Hosp    RENAIX, Sancta Maria Pensionale         J0846

 108 (Br) Gen Hosp    BRUSSELS, Hospital Brugman              J6059

 111 (Br) Gen Hosp    BRUSSELS, Hospital Militaire, Ave la Couronnes  J6452

   8 (Br) Gen Hosp    BRUSSELS, Hospital St. Pierre           J6154

  75 (Br) Gen Hosp    BRUSSELS, Hospital des Veillards        J581564

 101 (Br) Gen Hosp    HEVERLE, Nr. LOUVAIN, Institute de Sacre Coeur  J863555

  32 (Br) Gen Hosp    THILDONCK    (for Psychiatric Cases only)  J827651

 106 (Br) Gen Hosp    WAVRE NOTRE DAME, Institute des Ursulines  J7878

 109 (Br) Gen Hosp    DUFFEL, Maison St. Norbet               J7383

 Mily Hosp            ANTWERP, Belgian Mily Hosp              J686944
 (163 Fd Amb)


 HQ (Med) 11 L of C Area.
 10 Mar 45
```

Sheila's orders, March 1945, delivering the wounded

Sheila meets Canadian Provost Brownie Eccles, March 1945

Brownie (right) and friend on patrol, Belgium 1945

Sheila and Brownie, summer 1945.

Sheila and Brownie's "Ghent Mamma". Written in French on the back of the photo (translated): "An affectionate souvenir for my lovely little friend Sheila and her dear husband, 24 August 1945. Mamma."

CHAPTER 6
LETTERS FROM A LONELY HUSBAND:
1945 TO 1946

Letter writing was in Sheila's veins, part of the genetic makeup of the O'Carrolls. Since before the turn of the twentieth century it was how her father William had stayed in touch with his kin in Ireland and his sisters in America, and with his brother Thomas in South Africa until Thomas no longer replied and was lost forever. It was the only way to communicate with the family he knew he would never see face to face again. It was how Sheila's parents had communicated with her sisters when one by one they emigrated to New York City, and how they reached out to the rest of the family throughout the war, expressing their worry and their love woven through the descriptions of the mundane details of their everyday lives.

Sheila had begun writing letters as a child to her Irish aunts and her oldest sister Agnes in the USA, and later to her sisters Nora and Kathleen when they too left England. Throughout the war, her correspondence travelled regularly to all her siblings wherever they were stationed and to her parents back home at 122 Richmond Street. Her notes were newsy and cheerful, upbeat and humorous, and she rarely complained unless it came with a good dose of self-deprecation.

"I shall be so happy when I can get some jolly good English biscuits again. They seem to have run out here at our barracks and I can't stand the hard tasteless ones they give us in our rations. I suppose though it won't hurt me as I've become a little chubby with all the good Army food. Hahaha!"

Her handwriting was fluid and legible, her grammar and spelling flawless.

In contrast to Sheila's prolific lifelong letter writing, Brownie's only experience putting pen to paper began when he left Canada earlier in the war. He had no reason before that to write much of anything to anyone, and he was uncomfortable expressing himself in writing. He was a do-er, not a talker or a writer. He had been lonely for the almost four years of the war before he met Sheila, missing his family and his home, and he was shaken by his experiences in Italy. When the honeymoon prematurely ended with Sheila's illness, their happy months together quickly came to an end and loneliness once again hit Brownie with full force.

Sheila and Brownie's letters to each other began just two weeks after they were married. Back at his barracks, Brownie sat on his bunk and wrote a short note to Sheila, addressed to the 115 British General Hospital where she was still recovering from her kidney infection.

How are you feeling now darling? I hope that you will soon be out again and how I wish I were there with you. I get very lonesome. I have our wedding presents with me, and so if you get a chance you can pick them up, or if I get a chance I will take them to Ghent and leave them with the old lady at the café.

I got a telegram from home greeting us on our wedding, so I will take a chance in sending it to you in this short letter. I got a letter today from my brother George and he has to have an operation, so I hope that you don't.

So here's hoping that you are fine and I will see you soon and not in the hospital. This is something now for me to write to the same person two days in a row. So with all my love and that's a lot too darling and hope to hear from you soon.

Your beloved husband. XXXXXXXXXXXXXXXX

In the autumn of 1945, when she was back in Coventry after the war, Sheila's only way to communicate with Brownie across the English Channel in Belgium was by letters. She saved his letters to read and re-read, going back to savour his nuggets of affection as she looked forward to beginning her new life with her Canadian husband. She waited in anticipation for the arrival of the postman every day, and was rarely disappointed. There was not much else for her to do except wait for Brownie's notes and for the travel documents to get her to Canada. After the last six years of activity and the camaraderie of her ATS mates, the daily routine of life with her parents and counting her ration coupons paled in comparison. The arrival of a letter from anyone, but especially Brownie, was her excitement for that day.

One morning in early October 1945, Sheila rushed into the kitchen, waving a letter in her hand, to tell her parents that Brownie was on his way to Coventry for the first time. "Brownie's been granted a short leave! Finally you get to meet him!" she said. "You're going to love him. Listen to this," she continued as she read out loud, *I still love you more and more every day that we are apart . . . I can hardly wait till I get over there to see you . . . I think we can make one another very happy.* William and Nellie looked at their happy daughter and smiled.

It was a brief but joyful reunion for a couple of days, although it seemed to Sheila that as suddenly as he had been given leave to see her, it was over, and Brownie was returning to Belgium. She ripped open the scribbled note he had written on the ferry from Dover to Calais France, just hours after he had left her in Coventry, en route back to his posting in Brussels. It read, *I just wish that I could turn around right now and go back to you. Every time I think of you it makes the tears come to my eyes.* Sheila knew exactly what he meant; the tears were made half of love and half of loneliness.

A few days later, Brownie wrote again:

I get very lonesome to see you. I just came back from a show, which didn't help my being lonely any, for it was just like all the other shows. It ended with love and I couldn't think of anything but you, darling. I just wish that I could put in words and on paper just how I feel towards you. These are the nights that I miss you. I miss those cold feet and that warm heart. Sheila laughed at their ongoing joke. *He might not be a great writer,* she thought, *but he's said exactly the right thing here!*

The cold of Brownie's barracks in Belgium was a constant theme in his letters. *"I still love you more and more everyday. Can you keep warm these nights without me?"* he wrote on a November night as winter was setting in. Living in unheated quarters was adding to his misery, and a few days later Sheila read again, *It's so cold here I can hardly write. I think that I will be over there again shortly after Christmas. I rolled over last night in bed to put my arms around you but you weren't there.* Sitting at home on the bed she had slept in as a child, she felt so guilty for being much more comfortable, or at least warmer, and surrounded by people who loved her. Brownie's trips to Coventry were still only snatches of time, a few days of leave separated by weeks of letters, but each time he saw her, the evidence of their growing family, the baby she was expecting, brought him great joy.

As November began to move towards December 1945, Brownie was getting frustrated about the delays in returning to Canada. He wrote to Sheila, *"The boys were all talking about going home and I have to stay. If I had of been just a Lance Corporal I would have been home in Canada in December. I get very lonesome now since I came back from leave. It seems different than when we were apart before, so I hope that I can always feel this way for you. There is no girl like my Sheila in any country. I love you more than ever."*

His despondency grew as the time dragged on and his loneliness began to turn to restlessness. With dismay, Sheila shared his letter from December 3rd with her parents. *I won't be able to be with you for Xmas dear. I feel very lonesome and homesick to see you darling. I feel so bad that it wouldn't take much to make me go AWL and go over to see you. Maybe I'll go and get drunk, but I guess it wouldn't do me any good.*

"Whatever can I say to keep his spirits up?" she asked William and Nellie.

"You have to convince him this is just for a short time," her father urged. "You'll be together soon. Just let him know you're well and tell him about how much the baby is growing."

She quickly wrote back to him encouraging him in typical British style to "carry on" for a bit longer, and in his next letter she was happy to see that he wasn't saying anything more about going AWL. *It is terrible cold, enough to freeze the cars and jeeps and how I wish I had you here to keep me warm at nights. We are moving to Holland and from there we will move to England. I hope to be there by January 3.*

A few days later, though, Brownie's December 10th letter again brought a lump to Sheila's throat. *I went to see 'Mom' in Ghent. I stayed in the same room that you and I always stayed in and you have no idea just how I felt to go to bed there without you. I just felt like getting up and going home to camp.*

"He's miserable," Sheila told William. "I didn't realize until now how much he hates military life. I once hoped he would stay in the army because I loved it so much, but I know that's not possible now."

"He's a farmer," William tried to explain. "He'll always be a farmer and he needs to go home to the land. And it's pretty clear he needs you by his side, my girl, so that at least ought to make you happy. Write to him right now and tell him about the letter you got today saying that your name is in the queue to go to Canada. That ought to brighten things up for him."

Brownie wrote back immediately. *Was I ever glad to hear you might be going to Canada. Just don't fall in love with any of my brothers. I hope that you find things at home as I've been telling you and I hope that you don't expect to find everything there like they might have in the city.*

Sheila should have paid more attention to his understated but prescient comment. Things back at the farm in Mount Forest were not at all like "they might have in the city." She was optimistically naïve about her new life in rural Ontario and Brownie knew it.

This has been a long and lonely day for me." Brownie wrote on Christmas Day 1945. *"How I wish I could have been with you.* Sheila's holiday dinner was far from sumptuous, but it was shared in the warmth of the Richmond Street sitting room with people she loved, her parents and her sister Tess, and even her older brother Bernard and his wife had stopped by. No one mentioned this was likely the last Christmas she would spend with them for a long time. She would be in Canada before the baby was born and she knew she would miss the comfort of having her family close by.

Finally, in late January 1946, Brownie was told he was going home. He scribbled a quick note to Sheila. *We won't be here much longer. The day is tomorrow. So when you write to me you can write to my home address.* Excited as he was about going back to the farm and his family, it was tainted with leaving her behind. *"How I wish you were going with me,"* he added.

A rushed update followed a few days later, written from the deck of his troopship *The Acquitania*.

"Just a few lines to let you know I'm on the boat at Southampton and hope to move soon for Canada. I hate the thought of leaving you here. I see by the paper a married Canadian woman had her baby the day after she landed in Canada. By what I hear you might be going in February. They have hospitals on ships, so don't worry dear. I want to have you here with me as soon as possible and I will meet you at the station with both arms open. I don't know how I will get this posted— I'll try to get a civilian to take it off for me. I will see you soon in Canada. With love and happiness."

No more letters arrived until February 8th, after Brownie was finished crossing the Atlantic. Sheila grabbed the envelope from the postman, ripped it open and read the news from Brownie to her parents. "Listen to this," she said grinning.

"I got home fine and does it ever feel good. Do I ever miss you. All the rest of the family are just waiting to have you here with them, but not any more than I do."

"We'll drink a toast to the good news then, shall we?" said William. "And to a happy future in Canada for ye both."

Happy though he was to be home in Canada, Brownie missed Sheila more than ever now that they were even further apart. Describing a feeling which would become famous a few years later thanks to Hank Williams, he wrote to her, *"I get so lonesome I could cry,"* and then added his relief at being out of the military and back on the farm. *"I don't do very much work but it's still better than the Army."*

On February 12th, 1946, Sheila received two telegrams from Canada. One was from Brownie wishing her a happy twenty-seventh birthday and was followed a day later with a letter.

I suppose you feel a year older today. Everyday I look for mail from you. You have no idea how I miss you Sheila. I think and dream of you every night and sometimes it brings the tears. It will be one big happy day when I meet you in Toronto and have you with me then for good.

Sheila added the latest little envelope to the growing stack of letters from the husband she had seen so little. She tucked it carefully into the trunk she was packing with their wedding presents, some baby things, and other bits and pieces she had gathered for her new life in Mount Forest. What Brownie didn't know, but she would soon tell him, was that in addition to his telegram on her birthday, she'd also received instructions for her voyage to Canada. Sheila and her very obvious baby bump would be joining him in just a few weeks.

CHAPTER 7
COMING TO CANADA:
SPRING 1946

"Ah, it's a cold one today!" the postman said, shivering a little as he handed the mail to Sheila at the front door of 122 Richmond Street. "It looks like that important letter you've been waiting for has arrived." He hesitated for a moment on the doorstep, hoping she'd open the envelope then and there and he could share in whatever news it was. "Oh thank you!" she said, taking it and gently closing the door. It was February 12th, Sheila's twenty-seventh birthday, and while she didn't expect much of a celebration in terms of food or gifts, given rationing and shortages of everything, the good news she received that day more than made up for it. The Canadian Wives Bureau had finally sent her instructions on how and when to travel to Canada, and her departure date was just eight days away!

Enclosed in the letter were tags for her luggage stamped "*WANTED*" for the items she'd need during the voyage, and "*NOT WANTED*" for the bigger pieces to be stowed in the ship's hold until she arrived in Halifax. There was also a train ticket to Liverpool, and detailed instructions for transport to the docks where she'd find the *SS Letitia*, a hospital ship. Never a good sailor, and now more than six months pregnant, she was relieved to be assigned to a hospital transport, where she was more likely to be well cared for.

As her family crowded into the little Richmond Street sitting room to toast her future travels and good health, Sheila read out loud the instructions from the Wives Bureau, standing as if she was a commanding officer, a rather pregnant one, giving the troops their marching orders. "*You are allowed baggage of up to 500 lb.*," she declared in a pompous voice, "*which could include linen, silver and cutlery, baby carriages, baby cots, golf clubs, and small musical instruments.*" "I guess that means you'll have to leave the piano at home," quipped her father. They didn't have one. "Bloody hell, silver and golf clubs?" added her brother Bernard. "You'd think you were the lady of the manor! Do you suppose Brownie will need some golf clubs on his farm?" Their laughter at the silly instructions masked the sadness of Sheila's pending departure. William and Nellie had gotten used to having her at home for the last five months, the longest time she'd spent at 122 Richmond Street since she'd finished school almost ten years earlier. They were going to miss her cheerful chatter and the youthful energy she brought to their lives. Now that the day had finally arrived, they could no longer ignore the reality that they might not see her again or ever meet her baby.

Along with all the other instructions, the Wives Bureau had advised Sheila to be "*warmly clad*" for the ocean travel and to take a steamer rug or light blanket for the unheated train. Her Berthing Card was included in the travel package, assigning her to Deck C, Compartment 4, Berth 568. It was not the luxury of a private cabin, but she didn't expect one, and was used to communal living after the last six years in the ATS. In fact, Sheila had never had a room to herself; she had always been sharing with her sisters, or Mary Greenaway, or her military pals. She was looking forward to the company and support of the other women onboard facing the same unknowns.

William insisted on accompanying Sheila on the train to Liverpool to make sure she and all her belongings made it safely to the ship. "Ah Sheila," he told her with a shake of his head, "I'll not be sending my expectant daughter off on this big adventure without making sure you get there properly." She was happy to have his company. Nellie had to settle for kissing her goodbye in Coventry, though, as she was so disabled by arthritis that it was very difficult for her to leave the house. Sheila was not the first of their children to leave England, but that didn't make the farewells any easier.

"Have you got everything you need?" Nellie asked for the umpteenth time from the front door as she and Sheila watched William pack her big brown army trunk and other boxes into the taxi for the train station. "Did you remember your warm blanket and your gloves? It'll be chilly on that ship." Sheila nodded yes and held her fragile mother in a gentle hug. They both knew it was just talk to distract from the final goodbye. "Give our Brownie a big kiss for us, won't you. And send us a telegram as soon as you arrive. We'll be worried." Nellie waved until the cab turned the corner at the end of the street; then, hobbling on her cane, she turned back into the house and wiped the tears from her eyes. Sheila silently looked out the cab window, afraid she would cry if she looked back at 122 Richmond Street or if she tried to say anything to her father beside her. Of all her departures over the past seven years, this was by far the hardest.

When Sheila and William arrived at the Liverpool terminal a few hours later, it was bustling with women and children looking for their boarding gates and directions to the pier, and de-mobbed soldiers and sailors arriving and departing. It was a noisy place crowded with people saying their goodbyes or waving madly to greet arrivals. "I'll see ye off here then Sheila, my darlin'," her father said, wrapping her in a long hug as the hubbub swirled around them. "Don't worry about Mother and me. We'll be fine and we'll be over the pond to see ye and the baby before ye know it."

"Oh Dad," she whispered as she kissed his grizzled cheek; she then stepped up onto the double-decker bus to the port, taking a seat on the top level so she could get one last look at the city. The band on the platform was playing "Danny Boy" as the bus pulled away, and with a lump in her throat she continued to wave goodbye to her father as his figure got smaller and smaller. She didn't know it then, but it was the last time she would ever see her beloved Irish da'.

Sheila never returned to England. She must have known, deep inside, that it would be too hard for her to ever leave it again.

In June 1946, a few months after she arrived in Canada, Sheila received a letter from the mother of another new bride, Jill, who had travelled on the *SS Letitia* with her. Although they hadn't known each other until they met in Liverpool they had made the trip together and stayed in touch. The letter read:

"I guess you are wondering why I am writing to you, but Jill sent me on your letter. How are you and the little babe that must be there by now? Are you getting settled in that strange new country? Jill is doing fine; she bakes all her own bread and looks after the animals on the farm. Considering she was an office girl, it's not so bad is it? I do miss her, Sheila. She is my only chick and it nearly broke my heart when I left her at Liverpool. I was thankful to leave her with you. Somehow you did not seem a stranger and the last glimpse of you both on top of that bus will live in my memory forever. You were both smiling so bravely, and us others just had to see you go like that. Your pop was grand and we kept together until he left us at Gosford Green."

Sheila held the letter tightly to her chest and took a few deep breaths. Those words from a stranger brought back a rush of memories, as if she had just left Liverpool the day before. She remembered the band playing "Danny Boy," the feel of her father's rough cheek as she kissed him goodbye, and him bravely waving as the bus drove away.

The brown "coming-to-Canada" army trunk remained with Sheila for the rest of her life. It had rounded corners and leather straps and was made of a kind of pressed wood, not metal. Her name and military identification number were painted on the side. For more than thirty years, through every household move, it retained its travel labels, the ship's sticker saying "*SS Letitia*" and her destination printed in black paint. Decades after her arrival in Canada, when Sheila lent it temporarily to one of her sons for a coffee table, his girlfriend scraped off all the stickers. She was heartbroken. Those stickers had solidly attached her to her past.

When the *SS Letitia* finally arrived in Halifax on March 3rd, 1946 with its cargo of injured soldiers and war brides, Sheila was processed through Pier 21 with the other wives and their children. Her immigration documents approved and stamped, and now officially a landed immigrant, she boarded a train to Toronto where Brownie was to meet her. It was an interesting but strange voyage, seeing her new country for the first time through the train windows, the endless forests and lakes and rocks, and the occasional little towns in the snow and mud of later winter. It seemed to be largely uninhabited. "Everything is so far apart," Sheila marveled to her fellow traveller Jill. "It's all so wild!" Jill replied. "Don't you wonder what's waiting for us at the end of the trip?"

"Let's just hope our husbands will actually be there at the train station like they promised!" Another woman interjected loudly, and the women in the train car burst into laughter.

Sheila was just one of 27,000 war brides coming to Canada at the end of the war. Others went to the USA and even further away to Australia and New Zealand. They were young British and European women who had lived through the war years, met a soldier or sailor or airman from another country, and left their home to start a new life elsewhere. Some of these marriages failed. Some of the husbands didn't even bother to meet their wives on arrival. Some women were abused. Some wives turned around and went home. Most, like Sheila, stayed, worked hard to adapt, and built a new life.

Brownie had told Sheila that he lived on a hundred acre farm. And yes, they had horses, and yes, there were many bedrooms in the big farmhouse near Mount Forest. "Doesn't this sound like a wonderful place?" she had gushed to her army friends, picturing a bucolic scene of the rolling green hills in Ireland because that was the farm country she was familiar with. "Look at this big house," she marveled as she passed around the pictures sent by Brownie's sister. "Oh, how lovely! Lucky you!" was most often the response. "Ohhh, I'm jealous. Can you find me a handsome Canadian too?" some of the other ATS drivers had joked. Sheila had visions of riding a horse around the estate in her leather boots and jodhpurs like the lady of the manor, directing the workers who were tending the cattle and crops. That notion was a far cry from the reality which met her. Brownie had had a sense that she was expecting something different, but didn't know how to explain life in rural Ontario to a city girl who'd never even lived in a village. He'd made a brief and subtle reference to her exaggerated expectations of the family farm in his letter just before Christmas: "*I hope you don't expect to find everything there like they might have in the city*". He was a man of few words, much better at showing than telling.

It didn't take long for Sheila to discover how off-kilter and romanticized her expectations of her new life in Canada had been.

As the oldest son, Brownie's parents had always expected that he would take over the family farm until the war interrupted those plans. During the years he'd been overseas, by necessity his next-oldest brother George had taken on much of the workload and management of the farm and it made sense that he would carry on. Despite that, it was still understood by the family that Brownie would have his own farm on his return to Canada. It was all he had ever wanted and he planned that Sheila would be beside him.

If Sheila's vision of her future life on a farm was unrealistic, Brownie's family had an equally abrupt wake up when she arrived. She was not what they thought of as a farm wife. He had done the same inadequate job of explaining Sheila to his family as he did of preparing Sheila for the farm.

Brownie was waiting for Sheila when she arrived at Union train station in Toronto, joyful and with his arms open as he'd promised in his letters, eager to introduce her to her new home. He piled her big trunk and her boxes into the car for the two hour drive to the farm.

"Well, this is Mount Forest, finally!" Brownie said proudly to Sheila as they arrived at the little town in the grey March light. She took in the wide main street and the yellow brick buildings as they drove through, the big maple trees still bare of their summer leaves, and the slushy roads. "Aren't we going to stop?" she asked as he kept going.

"No, just a couple more miles to the farm," Brownie answered. "Everyone is waiting for you." It took only a couple of minutes to pass through Mount Forest, and then they were out in the country again, the farm houses set way back from the road, long distances between them across snowy fields. Finally, they turned into a long rutted driveway still bearing much of the winter's heavy snow. Brownie bounced the car over the potholes, dodged around a few rocks, and stopped in front of the brick house.

Sheila stepped out of the car just as the house door opened and a crowd of people came out to the front porch. "Mother and Dad, this is my wife Sheila!" Brownie announced proudly, his arm around her shoulders as a grinning older man in overalls stepped forward and grabbed her in a hug. "Well it's about time! Dinner's getting cold!" her father-in-law Scott laughed.

"You must be Brownie's dad," Sheila grinned. Just behind him stood a middle-aged woman, wiping her hands on her apron. "Hello, I'm Brownie's mother," she said with a reserved smile. She made no move to hug her or shake her hand. "I'm so happy to finally meet you all," Sheila said, smiling at the gang of brothers and sisters nudging each other out of the way to shake her hand. Brownie's youngest sister Mabel, age fifteen, whispered to her sister Ella, "She's so pretty!" She was awestruck.

Despite wartime clothing shortages, before she left Coventry Sheila had found an elegant and stylish black plush winter coat for her long trip. With her thick black hair rolled into a twist, her sparkling dark eyes and her red lipstick, she looked to Brownie's little sisters like she'd just stepped out of a magazine, despite her obviously pregnant belly. It was a good first impression. She was worldly, something quite different from the country girls in Mount Forest. Brownie's gregarious father Scott was thoroughly charmed from the first day. Brownie's taciturn mother Annie was less so.

"Sit down, sit down, and tell us all about your trip! That must have been something," Brownie's sister Evelyn said. Sheila took a chair at the kitchen table and looked around. There was no electricity, no indoor plumbing, and no phone in the farmhouse, but the big, warm room filled with laughing, excited people made her comfortable. Brownie's brothers tried their old jokes with the pretty new sister-in-law, and poked fun at the unusual expressions she used. "Oh isn't that lovely!" they mimicked her accent when Sheila remarked on the farmhouse. "Well, it IS lovely!" she said again just so they could laugh once more. She took their teasing in the good-natured way they intended, just as she had with her own big brothers at home, knowing it was their way to make her feel included.

It was only a couple of weeks after her introduction to her new in-law's that Sheila's first letter arrived; it was from her sister Agnes. She found a quiet corner in the busy farmhouse where she could tuck herself into a chair, alone for a change, to read again and again the comforting words and advice of her oldest sister.

I had an idea you'd like a letter from someone from home when you got to your new home. It's over twenty-two years since I first left home and I remember how awfully homesick I was at first, and how wonderful those first letters were.

I'm so glad you sent me the pictures of you and Brownie in civilian clothes. You both look like real people and such a handsome couple. I like the looks of Brownie, he looks "solid" and I believe you're well matched. I hope you'll be happy.

At first it will be rather trying for you to adjust to the new land and customs, and the food. And it will be equally hard for your relatives to get to know and understand you. The English are notorious for being hard to understand. They are naturally reserved and shy and they often hide their shyness by an attitude of aloofness. And the folks here don't seem to understand that. But I wouldn't worry about being liked if I were you; you have enough Irish in you to be liked anywhere. And the Irish are liked the world over.

Gee, I hope so, thought Sheila. *I guess I'll have to try to be more Irish! And if anyone is aloof, it's Brownie's mother, not me.*

If there was a definition of the ideal post-war Canadian housewife in 1946, it did not have Sheila's picture beside it. No one could say she didn't try hard, but she faced a steep learning curve, a culture shock, and a role which was just about the total opposite of the way she had lived her life up to that time. Being misinterpreted as aloof was not going to be her only challenge.

Sheila brought no culinary or domestic skills to her marriage. Growing up the ninth of ten siblings in a family where food was scarce or rationed, leaving home at eighteen to start a job and live as an independent woman in a boarding house, there was rarely an opportunity to learn to cook. One of the many things she had loved about the army was having good food and not having to worry about where it came from. She arrived in Canada knowing how to make a good cup of tea and a toasted cheese sandwich, but not much else.

Life in Canada after the war was expected to return to "normal". The men were back from fighting and were looking for jobs. Women who had temporarily taken over "men's work" were supposed to return to being housewives and mothers full time. Only husbands went to work and brought home a paycheque, while wives were expected to be happy staying at home and running the household. A good wife should have her lipstick on and a nice dinner ready when the man of the house arrived home from the office. Everyone wanted a return to peace and stability and the way things used to be. Those social expectations meant Sheila had to quickly adapt to a domestic role for which she was very much unprepared, and which had never actually been her ambition. She could easily change the oil in a truck or fix a flat tire, but she didn't know how to bake a pie. And if that wasn't enough, she was about to take on the responsibility of being a mother.

Her mother-in-law Annie had to start from scratch to teach Sheila how to care for her husband and household by Canadian farm wife standards. There was no written manual for Sheila to reference. It was a daunting challenge for both of them, and the bar was set high. Annie Eccles was an excellent baker and cook. There were always homemade muffins and biscuits on her table. There were hearty meat and potato meals, and homemade preserves and jams loaded with sugar.

The saving grace was that Brownie was a pretty decent cook himself and very handy with household tasks. Before the war he had enjoyed the times he spent at his mother's side, cooking on the kitchen woodstove, and he had honed his potato peeling skills on the troop ship to Europe. He wasn't likely to starve. He was equipped with lots of patience and an abundance of love for his wife, but he was shocked to realize just how little she knew about navigating the kitchen.

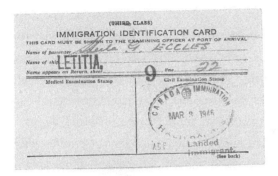

The "not wanted" tag for Sheila's army trunk to be stored in the hold of the
SS Letitia on her voyage to Canada.
The ship's card designating Sheila's accommodation on board.
Sheila's official Landed Immigrant stamp in Halifax, March 3rd, 1946, and
her train ticket to Mount Forest, good for a year until March 4th, 1947!

Sheila and Brownie, on the veranda of the Eccles farm, March 1945. She's hiding the baby bump beneath her fuzzy coat.

CHAPTER 8
THE LONG ROAD TO BECOMING A FARM WIFE: LATE 1940's

"Please darling," Sheila whispered, snuggled up to Brownie under her mother-in-law's hand-sewn quilts in his old childhood bedroom at the top of the stairs, "we need to find our very own place. After all these months of being apart, let's start our own home." Beside them in the other bedrooms, Sheila could hear the chatter of her new sisters-in-law and the horseplay of Brownie's younger brothers. It was hard to find any moments of privacy and quiet in his parents' farmhouse.

Sheila was used to living with others, her own siblings and her army friends, but this was all so new and different. A vast and cold country. A rural farm. A family with ways of doing things Sheila didn't always understand and which sometimes made her feel like an outsider, despite how kind they were. Even Sheila's body was not the same; it was growing bigger with a baby constantly kicking a visceral reminder that everything she once thought she knew had changed.

Their stay at the family farm lasted only a couple of weeks until Brownie found a little furnished apartment for rent in Mount Forest on the second floor of one of the old Main Street buildings. It was badly in need of repair and poorly equipped, but it provided them, especially Sheila, with some privacy and independence. "Oh, it's going to be lovely," she predicted enthusiastically, holding onto Brownie's arm as they looked through the small rooms. "What jolly good luck you heard about this!" She ignored the shabby furniture, the cobwebs, and dripping taps, and knew with some elbow grease she would have it cleaned up in no time. "You can fix that sagging cupboard door darling, can't you," she encouraged, "and put some nails in the floor where the board is loose, so we don't trip on it. George will help you." Brownie just smiled. As long as Sheila was happy he'd go along with it, but he knew his family's warm farmhouse was far more comfortable. It was going to be her first married home and Sheila was seeing a rosy view of it, rather than its limitations. Housing for returning veterans was hard to find, and they both knew they were lucky to get it.

What they really needed was a job and an income for Brownie. He was a hard and willing worker, but his opportunities were limited by his lack of education and experience beyond the family farm. Without a trade, competition for unskilled jobs was fierce. It didn't matter that he had served his country, so had the thousands of other veterans returning from the war, all of them now hoping to put that experience behind them and build a new life.

All Brownie had ever wanted to be was a farmer, and because of that, he saw finding a job as an interim measure at best. He wasn't interested in a career, just something to support them in the short term until he could find a property where they would live the rest of their lives. It was a simple dream. It was the only future Brownie could see for himself and his family, and he believed it was the remedy for the unease and restlessness he'd felt since returning to Canada.

"We'll get settled soon. I promise you," he tried to reassure Sheila. "If I have to go to Toronto for a while to earn some money I can stay with my sister Ev. It's just short term. As soon as I find my own farm, everything will be good. You'll see."

"Why don't you look into joining the Ontario Provincial Police?" Sheila prodded him repeatedly. "You have the background and experience, and you were good at being a provost. They'll be looking for men like you." The dashing man she had fallen in love with, in his smart military police uniform, carrying the respect and authority that went with it, had been replaced by a man in old work clothes, looking for a job and unsettled about the future. But for Brownie, the war years as a provost had been more than enough and he had no desire to continue policing. "Sheila, I don't want to do that anymore," he said. He resisted again and again. "I never liked it in the first place." He was happy that his younger brother George had taken on the responsibility of the family farm in his absence, and he was convinced that he could start afresh with his own. The federal government was offering financial incentives for WW2 veterans to return to school or to purchase lands and homes, and Brownie fully intended to take advantage of the assistance to get a farm. Sheila's preference was to use the veterans' funding for Brownie to return to school to advance his education or learn a trade, but he refused. It was the first but not the last time where their views of the road ahead sharply diverged.

All their plans for the future were overshadowed however by the most urgent event, the arrival of the new baby. The challenge of getting to know each other as a married couple in civilian life and the excitement of setting up their own home paled in comparison to the anticipation of the little person who was soon to be joining them. Sheila gathered up the things they would need, dozens of cloth diapers, glass baby bottles with rubber nipples, and the big pot to sterilize them, squeezing her limited funds to purchase the basics and ignoring anything frivolous or unnecessary. Her mother-in-law Annie found a basket and a used crib for later. Family and friends knitted blankets and little outfits and passed along the hand-me-downs from their own children. "Oh, it's ever so lovely!" Sheila found herself saying again and again, grateful as little gifts and baby things arrived to add to her small cache of supplies. Sheila had scrubbed their Mount Forest apartment from top to bottom and disinfected everything she could until the place smelled of bleach and Dettol. She was taking no chances. She knew nothing of babies except what she read, and she was determined to follow the advice in her books.

By late May 1946, the baby was about to arrive, and Sheila and Brownie were both a bit jittery waiting for something to happen. Brownie felt like the walls of their small apartment were closing in on him, but by then Sheila was too uncomfortable to do much more than sit and listen to the radio and wonder at the funny feeling in her belly. "I'm going to go up home for a while," Brownie announced to Sheila one evening, getting up from the kitchen table as soon as they'd finished eating dinner. "I'll go down to the barn and help with the milking." At least at the farm, Brownie convinced himself, he could feel useful. Sheila poured herself a cup of tea and nodded, recognizing his now familiar restlessness and his need to keep busy. She didn't want to go anywhere.

When he strolled into his mother's kitchen ten minutes later, Annie was surprised. "What are you doing here?" she said. After looking around, she continued, "Where's Sheila?"

"She's at the apartment. She doesn't feel very well. There's nothing much to do there so I thought I'd come out to help in the barn," Brownie replied.

His mother looked at him with her hands on her hips and the same stern, unsmiling face she had used when he was a child and had done something to earn her disappointment. Her disapproval was clear. "Your wife is about to have a baby," she said slowly, as if he needed this explained to him. "Any moment. You shouldn't be here. Get back there with Sheila right now and take care of her."

Their big, bouncing baby boy arrived that night, May 25th, 1946. Conceived in Belgium, his first few months of development spent in war-torn Coventry, he had crossed the ocean in the *SS Letitia* and half the country on a train before he was even born. He'd already done more traveling than many people do in a lifetime. They named him Randolph, after Winston Churchill's son, adding William for Brownie's first name and that of Sheila's father, and Hollick for Sheila's mother's family. William Randolph Hollick was a serious name, but he was Randy for short, a beautiful healthy baby with dark eyes and hair and olive skin. Among his blue-eyed Eccles cousins, he stood out as very much a little Irish O'Carroll.

"He doesn't look much like his dad," Brownie's brothers playfully joked to Sheila. "Are you sure there wasn't someone else hiding in the woodpile?" She laughed. Even their teasing couldn't dent the love she felt for her perfect boy.

One month after Randy was born, Sheila's older brother Bill wrote to congratulate her. He already had a daughter and knew how fiercely proud she was feeling.

Good going kid, and I know you'll be very happy and busy now. You'll feel life is something after all. The future might hold all the difficulties and worries imaginable but you've now got that something that will make you overcome all the snags.

After all the changes in her life over the last ten months, Sheila happily jumped into yet another new role as a mother. Unlike Brownie, who had helped with his younger brothers and sisters and seen lots of farm animal births, she had no experience with babies of any sort. It was one more set of skills she needed to master quickly, and it was far more important than baking a pie or even driving an ambulance. Closely following the directions of a government booklet *The Canadian Mother and Child*, she made sure to establish a firm routine for eating and sleeping. "It's his nap time," she said when Brownie suggested they pack Randy up and go to the farm. "He can't go now." She was constantly wiping off counters and disinfecting the diaper pail, vigilant that her Randy-boy stay safe from the dangers she could see as well as the ones she couldn't. In the wide range of advice she received from family and friends, she chose what she would accept and what she would ignore, preferring to lean in the direction of the published experts. Sheila may never have pictured herself washing dozens and dozens of cloth diapers every week or carefully measuring and sterilizing baby formula every day, but she loved it.

Unfortunately, other parts of Sheila's life were not so idyllic. With no jobs in Mount Forest, Brownie had to take work away from their home, often coming back only on weekends. Money was extremely tight. Together barely a few months, they were forced to live apart again most of the time. It was hard to adapt to a new life as a family when everything remained so unsettled. For Brownie, it was too much like the time on his own in Belgium just after they were married, and he was very lonely and unhappy again without his little family. For Sheila, it was long days alone with a new baby in a country she didn't yet understand.

1946 and then 1947 slowly passed with nothing permanent in sight for them. Brownie worked at whatever he could find while he searched for a suitable property and waited for the slow wheels of the Veterans Land Act administration to review his application for a farm purchase. "There's just no decent farms around for sale," he lamented repeatedly to Sheila. Staying with his sister Evelyn and her husband Bill in Mimico, he took a factory job he hated. Inside a hot building all day, listening to the clank and roar of machinery, Brownie dreamed of a future when he would work outside in his fields. When that job ran out, he worked in a feed meal, a construction site, and a road building crew. Meanwhile, Sheila remained in Mount Forest in the shabby little apartment with baby Randy, trying to keep him happy and healthy and safe and eager to get on with their life together on the long awaited farm. It was not always easy for either of them.

One quiet afternoon as Randy was napping, Sheila turned from washing bottles in the sink to find a stranger standing in her kitchen. Startled, she shrieked, waking Randy who began to howl. The unkempt old man who lived in the apartment down the hall had opened her door without knocking and shuffled in uninvited. "Thought I'd come by for a cup of tea," he said, toothlessly grinning as if they were old friends and this was normal. "I knew you were all by yourself."

"No," Sheila said, her voice quivering, as she moved him toward the door and away from the baby, "you can't come in." She closed it firmly behind him and turned the flimsy lock. She was shaken by the intruder and horrified that he had assumed he could enter uninvited. She didn't trust the lock and worried she would wake up one night to find him by her bed, or worse, by Randy's. When she recounted the episode to Brownie that weekend, he immediately went down the hall to set the old man straight. Whatever he said worked, and there were no more surprise visits. Just the same, after that frightening encounter, before she went to bed every night Sheila pushed a heavy dresser against the door. "I worry about what happens if there's a fire and how quickly we could escape," she told Brownie, "but I worry more about that disgusting old man."

With Brownie's income undependable and erratic, Sheila scraped along as best she could. Sometimes there was nothing in her purse if Brownie's pay hadn't arrived. "*I'm sorry about asking George to help out with some money,*" she wrote to Brownie, "*but the rent was due and you know how I hate to owe money. I hope you're not too upset with me and I'll try not to do it again.*"

Sheila was desperately homesick and just as desperately trying to hide it. All her communication with her parents back in Coventry and with her brothers and sisters in the USA and around the world was by post. Phone calls were unreliable and restrictively expensive, reserved for emergencies only. Weeks could go by without a letter from her family or old army friends. Sheila felt confined in her apartment, isolated in her new country and worried about the future for her baby boy. She didn't even have a car to allow her to visit the few local friends she had made. In those cold winter days of early 1947, as she passed the long hours alone listening to the radio, she chanced upon a commentator from the BBC named Patrick Lacey. In the familiar and comforting British radio announcer voice Sheila missed hearing, he talked about the every day lives of ordinary English people. To Sheila it sounded so much better than her current situation and she immediately wrote to him inquiring about the possibility of farming in England.

Patrick Lacey's handwritten reply, on flimsy blue airmail paper, was dated February 14th, 1947. Sheila grabbed it from the mailbox with a big intake of breath, her heart pounding. She hadn't really expected a response, especially not so soon! She quickly tucked Randy into his crib and tore the envelope open, sinking onto one of the worn kitchen chairs to read it.

Dear Mrs. Eccles: I have only just received your letter in the last half hour, so this is not an attempt to answer it yet. I only want you to know as soon as possible that I'm extremely sorry for you (and your husband) and will write again more fully when I've had time to think things over, make some inquiries, and so on. I want to help you as much as I can, one way or another.

Just at present, of course, it is astonishing for me, here in England, that anyone who has escaped from England should want to return to it, for since you wrote we've fallen into a fine mess. Even before this new crisis, many men and women coming out of the Forces were surprised and dismayed at finding out how much harder life in Civvy Street was. And your husband is right in thinking that farmers and farming here are under a big dose of Government control. At the same time I can understand the feeling you have for the English scenes and environment of English social life; I used to get the same feeling, now and then, during my eight years in India, so I'll tell you as soon as possible everything I know, and everything I can find out.

I'm quite sure you would be wiser to "stick it out" in Canada if you can but equally I'm ready to help you in case you can't.

Yours sincerely, Patrick Lacey.

PS: There are very many farms and villages in England that have no electricity at the best of times!

Sheila dropped the letter and put her head in her hands, ashamed and sad and despairing all at the same time. "How could I be so stupid?" she said to the emptiness in the apartment. "As if we'd be going back to a farm in England!" Her loneliness and sheer desperation were so obvious that Patrick Lacey had felt he had to reply immediately and offer help. She thought she could placate Brownie's dreams by offering a farm in England, an idea Brownie always argued against, and she had hoped the voice on the radio could help her convince him. She had poured out her heart to a total stranger, grasping for a lifeline that wasn't there. It was heartbreaking to accept the reality that returning to the UK was not an option. She carefully put the letter in a drawer so Brownie wouldn't find it, then straightened her back as always, and went back to washing diapers.

The unsettled hand-to-mouth existence dragged on, and Sheila continued to be alone much of the time with Randy in Mount Forest. Ten months after her correspondence with Patrick Lacey, she had stopped revealing, at least to Brownie, any more evidence of her worry. Only her grit and stiff upper lip were evident as she made the best of things despite the hardships, and her letters to Brownie were unfailingly upbeat and cheerful, reassuring him that there was a light at the end of the tunnel.

On the evening of December 16th, 1947, Sheila was sitting in her little kitchen with a cup of tea in the middle of writing another letter to Brownie when an unexpected phone call from him interrupted her. They talked about the possibility of Sheila joining him in a place he'd found for rent in Cooksville, and when she hung up the phone she went back to her letter writing.

It's not easy to talk on the phone; one sounds so formal, but I was very happy to hear your voice and I think I've missed you about ten times more than you could imagine. So hurry up Xmas and come and see Randy and me and then we'll be really happy.

The place near Cooksville sounds OK, but as you say I won't think too much about it till we're there. Forgive the next little request—you know me and my funny ways. Thank heaven you do! Well, darling, when you next visit the place, could you furtively place some of my pet "mice die for it" seeds down—just in case! Then I'll feel at ease. Don't forget angel, will you?

It's not so good being apart like this, is it? I won't let it happen again—unless it's hols or anything like that—but not having a home together is the worst thing we could ever do. However, it's all very good for one to experience these things, eh?

Sorry I was out the Saturday evening you phoned, but I can never kill the time we're apart moping at home, so I was out with the girls. That way the time gets nearer and nearer till I see you. Otherwise it would drag awfully.

Sheila couldn't stop thinking about the idea of moving to Cooksville, and before the week was over she sat down again to put her feelings on paper. She wanted Brownie to understand how enthusiastic she was for them to be together.

Whatever it is, I'm very keen to get cracking and fix it up, because this living apart is no d... good is it? Now that I've had a little experience in that sort of thing, fixing up I mean, I think we can make anywhere over into a home. So long as we're together that's the main thing, and we'll just have to make everything as nice as we can—sort of improvise like Army days, eh?

As for you, you know I miss you like the devil, so be of good cheer.

Finally, several months later and after two long years of uncertainty, Brownie's prayers for a farm were answered. In mid-1948, he found what he thought was the perfect property for sale. It had fifty-nine acres including a woodlot, a nice brick farmhouse, a big barn, and some outbuildings. If he could somehow manage to scrape together enough to satisfy the asking price of $4800, it would be his. It was a huge amount of money for a veteran with no savings.

The first challenge was to get the financing approved through the Veteran's Land Act, but after all the waiting and hoping for a farm property, the separations and the loneliness, his application for funding was summarily denied. The small farm didn't quite meet the minimum size of tillable acres required, he was told in a perfunctory letter.

"I don't know what to do next, Sheila," Brownie said with tears in his eyes when he read the letter, overwhelmed by the setback. "I thought it was the perfect place for us. I don't know if I can start the search all over again." Sheila was not ready to let Brownie give up and have to endure more months of living in limbo until they found another farm, if they even could. "We can fight this!" she insisted. "There has to be a process for appeal." Not about to passively take no for an answer and not intimidated by a bureaucratic process, she immediately started to research how to find a way around this roadblock. Relying on the things she'd learned working in the bank a decade earlier, she prepared the facts and figures they needed to argue their case. "We've got nothing to lose," she said, putting the neatly prepared document in front of Brownie and handing him the pen to sign it. "You can show them this will work. I've got the analysis right here." The next morning she took it to the post office in Mount Forest and watched as the postmaster dropped it into the outgoing bag.

They didn't have to wait long for a response. In short order a letter arrived from Veterans' Affairs advising Brownie to appear for an interview in Guelph. Armed with Sheila's arguments and figures, and in his own quiet dignified way, Brownie convinced them he was willing and able to make a go of this farm. There weren't a lot of properties available, but there was a long list of veterans looking, so an exception was granted and the mortgage approved.

Brownie was thrilled. Sheila was proud and relieved, and for the first time since her arrival in Canada, felt empowered.

The deed was made out in Brownie's name only. Sheila, like other wives in that era, was not considered the owner, regardless of what she contributed.

While the future looked brighter as she took the next step into her life in Canada, Sheila had no way to know this shaky start to Brownie's farming aspirations did not bode well.

Sheila and Brownie, circa 1947

CHAPTER 9
IS THIS COUNTRY LIFE?:
1948 TO 1954

The long-sought farm was situated so far down a rutted gravel side road that even the mailman didn't come by. The rural mailbox, Sheila's primary contact with her family and the rest of the world, was a ten-minute walk from the farmhouse, perched on a crooked fencepost at the intersection of their rough side road with the townline. When she arrived at the mailbox, if she turned left onto the township road, it was a few more miles to the Eccles home farm and then a bit further to Mount Forest. If she turned right at the mailbox, the township road led to a paved highway and then on to Palmerston. There was only one other farm on their side road; it sat up a very long driveway directly across the road.

Sheila's new home was a big square Georgian style farmhouse built of yellow brick. It was a bit of a faded lady since not much had been done to update it over the years, but it still had a lot of charm. A substantial staircase led from the front entry to the second floor where four bedrooms opened onto a gallery around the stairs. Another steep and narrow set of stairs in one of the smaller bedrooms led to the dusty unfinished attic. Old boards had been laid loosely across the beams to form part of the floor, but one missed step and an attic visitor could crash through into a bedroom below.

On the main floor, one entire side of the house was taken up by the large kitchen. Across the central hall, the living room and what was intended to be a formal dining room took up the other side. Sheila immediately decided the smaller room would be a playroom for Randy. "Why do we need a dining room?" she asked Brownie. "We don't even have a dining room table yet." Much to Sheila's delight the house had electricity, unlike her in-laws' farm. There was no running water, but the kitchen had a hand pump. There was no flush toilet, but there was a small room off the kitchen set aside as a wash room, and there was an outhouse behind the woodshed. It was definitely more primitive than what she had been used to in England, but many times larger than her parents' home. 122 Richmond Street could have fit into Sheila's new farmhouse twice, with room left over.

The damp and cobwebbed cellar with a dirt floor was used for storing winter vegetables. As Sheila went down there to grab some potatoes for dinner, she cheekily quipped to Brownie, "I'm going down to the Suez Canal." It was a reference to the current political tensions in the Middle East, which she was following closely on the news because her brother Patrick was there working in the oil fields. It was also a broad hint to Brownie that she wanted him to fix the water running through the foundation stones when it rained. "I'll try to get that done in the winter when it's dry," Brownie assured her. Like all farmhouses, there was a large woodshed or summer kitchen attached to the back of the house; it was the unimpressive entrance that everyone used in true Canadian farmhouse tradition. The more elegant front door, which opened into the central hall, was rarely opened. It was a typical Ontario farmhouse, but a rather nice one with its pine trees ringing the large front lawn. They swayed and sighed in the wind like whispers of welcome. Their new home even came with a collie dog named Tippy.

Sheila stood on the back stoop the day they moved in, taking a private moment away from unloading boxes and cleaning cupboards to look out over the fields and the woods stretching away. *Finally we have our own home,* she thought, even though it was not quite like her early expectations of her life on a Canadian farm. She smiled to herself remembering her naïve notions of the jodhpurs, the riding horse and the tenant farmers, like an early 20th century grand estate in England. *It wasn't all that long ago,* she thought, *but it was such a different world.* She was thrilled and eager to take on the challenges of this new life with Brownie, even though she was worried about the huge debts they had acquired. They were both just twenty-nine years old, had seen and done a lot of interesting things in their lives so far, and were enthusiastic about starting to build a stable future together. Finally.

She quickly took some pictures with their old camera to capture the excitement of moving day, but it was weeks later when she finally got the film into the drug store to be developed. On the back of one of the snaps she jotted "*Our new permanent home—ten miles from Mt. Forest. Very wild looking at the moment; just moved in!*" and mailed it to her sister Agnes.

The picture of the farmhouse Sheila mailed to her sister Agnes.

Randy and dog Tippy in front of Sheila and Brownie's farmhouse,
circa 1949.

Sheila was thrilled to be settling into a permanent home, even if she was a little overwhelmed at the enormity of what they had taken on. It was a big house to fill, and they had little in the way of household goods or furnishings, but she was frugal and creative and keen to make a home from the bits and pieces they picked up second hand or at auctions. "Let's bid on that oak table," she encouraged Brownie in an urgent whisper, gripping his arm at her first estate sale. "I love the curvy lion's claw feet. See if you can get it!" Brownie had experience with auctions and knew they had to be patient. "Hold on," he said quietly. "Don't start the bidding. Try not to look too excited." It worked, and by the end of the sale, he was happy to load up Sheila's new treasures to take home. They were glad to get hand-me-down furniture and dishes from friends and family, the way most couples began their married lives post-war. There was a shortage of manufactured household goods anyway, even if they'd had money to buy things brand new.

Always concerned about germs and in particular bedbugs, Sheila scrubbed every piece of used furniture top to bottom before it was allowed to enter the house. She waged a constant war with the flies from the barnyard and the vermin that liked to sneak in through the cracks and crevices in the old house, and she enlisted Brownie to do the fighting.

"Brownie, there's another mouse in the trap!" she shrieked at least once a week, too disgusted to remove the dead body herself. "I'll get it," Brownie responded patiently each time.

"Please Brownie, would you be a dear and hang some new fly stickers above the kitchen sink? These are loaded with dead ones." Brownie climbed the step stool and carefully replaced them.

"Brownie, don't come into the kitchen in those barn clothes!" she barked, "and leave your mucky boots in the woodshed". He didn't need reminding, but he didn't complain. Best to stay silent.

She made sure the well water was tested regularly. Her lovely little boy Randy was not going to be put in any risk if Sheila could help it.

Everyone in the O'Carroll family seemed to think Sheila's jump into farming was a grand idea, even though none of them had ever been, or would ever be, farmers themselves. It had a romantic charm to it (if you ignored the hard work), and Sheila and Brownie were often the recipients of their praise and questions and unsolicited advice. And their visits.

To Sheila's sister Agnes in particular, the farm was a source of constant fascination and scientific interest, and she didn't hesitate to offer her opinion and theories on most of its operations. As an officer and a nurse in the US Army, she was quite used to giving orders and expected them to be followed, especially by her younger siblings. Sheila looked up to her as an expert in just about everything. In reality, Agnes was a bossy big sister, but Sheila both adored her and was a little afraid of her.

Relaxing at the kitchen table after dinner, the meal finished and the dishes waiting to be washed, Sheila read to Brownie the most recent letter from her older sister and the bits of farming advice it contained.

"Brownie, Agnes says we should test our well water every month."

"Brownie, Agnes sent me an article about pig diseases. You should read it."

"Brownie, Agnes wants to know if you'd like some more of that salve for your hands the next time she comes."

As always, Brownie listened and nodded in his noncommittal way, and went on doing what he was doing.

It was a hot day in August 1949, about a year after they'd been on the farm. Sheila pulled open the mailbox door, squeaking on its rusty hinges, expecting only the usual pile of overdue bills, and was pleasantly surprised to find a letter from Agnes. She had just left the farm a few days earlier after her first visit and was eager to share her observations.

You know Sheila, I really envy you. You have a lovely farm and it has wonderful possibilities. I enjoyed my visit immensely and look forward to visiting you again next year and hope I can stay for a month next time.

I can't believe you dared to try to milk a cow, more power to you. I can understand men being in a hurry at chow time and not showing you much, but that comes with time and you will gradually be able to give a hand as needed without being told what is expected.

Sheila smiled to herself at the reference to milking, and remembered the laughs she'd shared with Agnes just a week earlier in the barn as she'd tried, unsuccessfully, to get milk from that Holstein. She shoved the letter into her apron pocket and promised herself she'd read it again, carefully, when she had a few quiet moments.

Despite her best efforts and willingness to try most farm chores, and even with Agnes's encouragement, Sheila quickly realized that barn work was not her strength. The two old draft horses, the pigs and chickens, and the herd of cows remained solely Brownie's domain. "I'll drive the tractor," she volunteered enthusiastically, "you'll need someone to do that." With her experience driving trucks in the army, she quickly mastered its difficult operation. At the same time, she worked hard to keep the household running, despite having few modern conveniences, and to do the things that farm wives were expected to do, right down to making pickles and feeding the big gangs of neighbours who came in to help with haying or threshing.

"Sheila, " Brownie said carefully on the first morning of haying as he left for the fields, "Have the dinner ready on the table waiting when we come in. Please." He knew that being late was an O'Carroll trait she shared with her whole family, and there was a big risk that his hungry helpers would have to wait for their meal when they came back to the house at midday. He was right. Much as she tried, Sheila couldn't quite get the hang of it. The hot and tired farmers wanted to get the job done and get home, but instead found themselves waiting at the kitchen table for Sheila to get the meal to them. "It's coming," Sheila sang out to the assembled dusty men as she banged the pots on the stove and hurried to dish out the potatoes. "Just two shakes of a lamb's tail!"

Distinguished guests always arrive late. Sheila remembered her mother's often used explanation for being tardy, deployed as a rule rather than an excuse. "I guess that doesn't apply to farmers," she mumbled to herself as she wiped the sweat from her forehead. She cleaned up the remains of the meal as the men trooped back to the haying, and couldn't resist a laugh at herself. *Imagine the complaining when those men get home about that English woman who couldn't get it right.*

By the autumn of 1951, however, Sheila was finally feeling more confident and comfortable with her new life, and in almost every letter to her younger sister Tess in Coventry, she tried to convince her to move to Canada.

This place grows on me more than ever tho we have many problems too. I seem to have got better organized all around and can see so many of the finer sides of life out here.

This being fall one can appreciate whether the summer's work has been balanced off by the harvest or not. It has been fairly good all round. My little vegetable garden has been useful too, and I did a lot more canning this year. Pickled beets, tomatoes, cucumbers, cherries, peaches, pears, and plums were all put down in the cellar and that helps the winter budget no end.

I often get crazy ideas that you might get over here and we'd do a whole lot of canning together.

1951 had been a busy year for Sheila, and when she stood in the musty cellar to admire her rows and rows of preserves, she mentally ticked off another hard-earned accomplishment in her new life. She had done all this work with a new baby as well as a five-year-old under her feet. Just a year earlier, in August 1950, she had given birth to a big baby girl. They named her Simonne, after a wartime friend in Belgium. Blue eyed and very fair, she was the opposite of her older brother Randy and the darling of her dad.

As Sheila bathed Simonne in a tub by the kitchen woodstove she sang an old pre-war song. *Mares eat oats and does eat oats and little lambs eat ivy. A kid'll eat ivy too, wouldn't you?* Simonne giggled and splashed the water.

"Ohhhh, my little lambsy-divey," Sheila cooed as she wrapped Simonne in a towel she had warmed on the back of the stove. "Let's get you all cleaned up for Daddy." These were idyllic moments for mother and daughter.

There were long stretches of time when Brownie was in the barn or the fields and Sheila was on her own in the house with the children. As always, she passed the hours with the radio on, her constant companion the CBC, keen to keep up with world affairs and new farm techniques to urge on Brownie. "I heard this on the farm report today, Brownie," was often Sheila's conversation starter at dinner. Brownie nodded but said nothing. He had far more experience at farming than Sheila, and while he appreciated her enthusiasm, he wasn't interested in changing the way he'd been taught to do things. Pasteurization became her favorite topic; it was something she heard a lot about on the radio. It was a very timely and personal issue because it directly affected her own children. Sheila didn't want them to drink raw milk straight from Brownie's cows.

Each evening Brownie brought the warm milk up from the barn to the kitchen, directly from the cow and his hands. Sheila then strained it through cheesecloth to remove any foreign matter. "This doesn't get rid of the micro-scopic germs," she complained to Brownie, repeating what she had learned on the CBC. He was not convinced. "I drank fresh milk all my life," he replied. "And it didn't hurt me. I don't know why you bother." Sheila dismissed his opinion and insisted that any milk her children drank had to undergo a home pasteurization process. Painstakingly following the procedure recommended in the farm report, she boiled and cooled all the milk before she allowed Randy or Simonne to drink it.

The facts were on her side of the argument. For decades scientists knew that raw milk can contain salmonella and e-coli and could spread tuberculo-sis. In 1927, a typhoid epidemic linked to raw milk had affected 5000 people in Canada. Finally, in 1938, the Ontario government had introduced legislation requiring compulsory pasteurization of any milk sold commercially, but it didn't apply to farmers consuming their own products.

Up the road at Brownie's parents' farm, science was ignored. They scoffed at the necessity to change what they had always done and saw no need to pasteurize. When Brownie took Randy and Simonne "up home" without Sheila, they were encouraged to drink the raw milk. "Your mother will never know," their grandfather Scott leaned in to whisper, as if it was a fun secret. The children looked over at their father for approval, but Brownie just shrugged his shoulders and said nothing either way. To the Eccles family, this was just one more in the list of sometimes amusing and often eccentric ideas that set Sheila apart. To Randy and Simonne, drinking the raw milk felt like disobeying their mother. It was a confusing betrayal.

Living on a dirt road far out in the country with no immediate neighbours and just the CBC for company most of the day, Sheila was more isolated than she had been in her little apartment in Mount Forest. At least there she had the opportunity for chance encounters with people on a walk to the post office or an occasional cup of tea with one of the women she'd met. On the farm, there was no one to chat with except Brownie, who was usually working in the barn and generally wasn't much of a conversationalist anyway. Visitors were very infrequent, except for the occasional stop by a travelling salesman.

One day the Rawleigh man knocked on the door, his big sample case in his hand, hoping for a new customer for his cleaning and medicinal products. "I heard someone new had bought this old farm," he said when Sheila came to the door. "Can I interest you in anything I have here?" Sheila invited him in. "I'm just making a cup of tea," she said. "Would you like one while I look at your catalogue?" She kept him chatting for much longer than he had planned to stay, but he left with a big order and gave her some samples to try. A few days later, stopping in at another farmhouse on his route, he met yet another war bride. This was where Joyce Bridge and her husband Bob lived with their baby boy. "You're the second war bride I've met this week!" the salesman said as she too invited him in. He asked if she happened to know the other English woman in the big farmhouse. "No, I don't," Joyce said.

"I've met a few other girls in Palmerston from back home, but I don't know anyone named Sheila."

"That's too bad. I think she's a bit homesick," he offered. "She must be very lonely back there on that isolated farm. I bet she'd love to see another gal from England." When he left, he gave Joyce vague directions to Sheila's farm "just in case."

"Let's see if we can find her!" Joyce urged Bob that night when she told him the story. "It'll be a jolly good adventure!" The next Sunday, they packed up their baby and went for a Sunday drive to see if they could find this lonely woman. They didn't know Sheila or Brownie, but they had the salesman's directions to the farm. They turned up what they hoped was the right driveway and got out of the car.

"Helloo! I thought you might like to hear another English voice," Joyce said, a big smile on her face, when Sheila and Brownie came out, surprised to see strangers knocking on their door. Sheila beamed back and invited them in. "I'm putting the kettle on," she said, and reached up in the cupboard for the best china teacups.

It was the start of a life-long friendship.

Through Joyce, Sheila soon met several other local war brides, forming a group they called "The Overseas Club." It was their link to a home far away, to a shared culture and the experience of immigrating. It was a listening ear and sometimes a shoulder to cry on or a voice to laugh with when things became overwhelming. They met every few weeks in each other's homes, summer and winter. Nothing stopped their gatherings, and they even drove through snowstorms to get to a meeting when they had to. They organized Christmas banquets together with their favorite English treats and held birthday parties for the kids. Some of the women had married farmers, some were married to businessmen, some to retailers. One was married to the postmaster. Some were well off, but most were not. They came from every social stratum in the UK, but in Canada, no one really cared. The class distinctions from before the war no longer existed. When they got together, the chatter and laughter of their dozen English voices sounded like a happy flock of chattering birds.

"You're so beautiful," little Simonne sighed, standing in her pajamas as she watched her mother get ready for the Overseas Club. Sheila's hair was freshly washed and rolled back, and with her lipstick on, she had magically morphed into someone pretty, wearing her nicest blouse with the cameo pin at her neck and the suede pumps that only came out from the back of the closet on special occasions. She didn't look at all like the ordinary mother her children were used to. "Be good for your daddy," Sheila instructed cheerily as she kissed Randy and Simonne good night. "I'll see you in the morning. Ta ta!" The stimulation of sharing those hours with other women so much like her would spill over into the next few days and the smile on Sheila's face would remain. The Overseas Club was a lifesaver. Finally Sheila had a way to bridge the gap between her old life and the reality of her new one.

CHAPTER 10
THE DEMISE OF THE FARM:
1954

"Brownie!" Sheila fumed, slapping yet another overdue bill on the table in front of him. "What did you do now? You told me you'd paid this." She jabbed her finger at him as her worry and frustration spilled out. "How am I supposed to look people in the eye when we owe them money?" Brownie sighed. "I had to buy the new tire for the tractor. Have you forgotten?" They'd had a version of this same argument over and over again almost since they'd started the farm.

"*Never a borrower or a lender be,*" Sheila chanted her parents' mantra to Brownie for the umpteenth time. "It's the never-never plan," she went on. "Never never paid for. Instead of debt, you make do until you've saved enough to buy the things you want."

"That doesn't work on a farm," Brownie told her again, his patience growing thin. "We can't wait to save that much money. We need to buy equipment, and animals, and feed before we can make any money to save."

The red side of their farm ledger continued to grow and Sheila worried constantly about whether they'd be able to pay the mortgage as well as all the other bills that seemed to roll in with no end in sight. She had taken on the bookkeeping role in the farm operation because she was good with numbers, but mostly because she didn't trust Brownie to stay on track. "What's this bill for?" she questioned him. "You took out a loan for those pigs? I thought you paid the farmer from the egg money!"

Brownie shook his head. "There wasn't enough and we needed chicken feed." And then, in a quieter voice, he added, "and I don't think I should have to ask your permission for everything I do."

As their money arguments escalated, Brownie became more secretive, borrowing without talking to her first, and "forgetting" to give her a bill he thought he could quietly pay later without her knowing when he'd sold a calf or a pig. "I'm going to the barn," he said more often in the evenings after dinner when the subject of unpaid bills came up again. "I've got something I have to finish there," he added, and he slipped out the door to avoid the confrontation.

"You can't always just walk away! It won't solve the problems!" Sheila yelled as the door closed behind him.

She dropped into a kitchen chair, put her hands over her face, and tried not to scream. *He doesn't understand that I lay awake at nights worrying about our debts,* she thought. *When do we start to see a profit?* She knew full well that their farm was a business, not a hobby, and she understood it required a huge amount of hard work from both of them, day in and day out. She was ready and willing for that part. Sheila was prepared to help him in whatever ways she could, but it was the financial risk taking where they saw things very differently.

Fortunately for Brownie, he had an ally in his sister-in-law Agnes. She had watched them struggling to get the little farm she so admired on a firm footing, and decided to step in. If anyone could convince Sheila that they needed to put more money into the farm, it was Agnes.

Knowing Brownie and Sheila would never accept a gift of money, Agnes offered instead to lend them some. Constantly worrying about their financial situation, Sheila swallowed her pride and agreed, despite the humiliation of taking money from her older sister. "Only if it's a formal loan agreement. It has to be in writing," she insisted to Brownie. "We don't want charity from Agnes regardless of how kind she is. We're going to pay it all back." He agreed. The loan was for $1000, a huge amount of money in the early 1950s, and more than twenty percent of the actual purchase price of the farm. Agnes's cheque was made out in Brownie's name only, but in her covering letter to Sheila, she spelled out her terms.

You may repay the loan in any amount you wish and over any period of time convenient to you. Please understand I have absolutely no desire to make any profit or interest in such a deal. Tell Brownie I admire his personal integrity and perseverance and I'll bet his practical experience and native intelligence could run rings around all the learned PhDs and theorists. What this world needs is more farmers and men who are not afraid to put a shoulder to the wheel.

Agnes said nothing about Sheila's contribution or the challenges she too faced, as if she was only a bit player in the drama that Agnes was watching from the sidelines.

Brownie wanted to be more than just a subsistence farmer like his father had been and his goal was a profitable dairy operation. In 1951, he began building a herd through the Canadian Jersey Cattle Club, buying registered pedigree animals. The records of their breeding could be traced back generations. "This is a good long-term investment Sheila," Brownie assured her. "Jerseys are good milk producers and they live a long life. We're going to start seeing some money come back to us soon."

"I hope you're right," Sheila said. "Everything we have depends on those cows." She knew nothing about the science of it, but strongly hoped this would be the springboard to moving their finances into the black ink side of the ledger.

As Brownie's herd began to grow, so did his confidence in his animals, and he decided to start competing at the local fall fairs. "We need to have some recognition of the quality of our heifers so we can do more breeding. It's the right time, and I think I'll do okay," he told Sheila. Sheila was enthusiastic to finally have some positive outcomes from all their work and worries. "That's exciting! It will be fun." And as he had hoped, Brownie began to win some prizes. A growing row of red and blue ribbons adorned a wall in their barn and, more importantly, his wins were officially registered with the agricultural society.

Encouraged by his success, in the summer of 1953 Brownie asked Randy if he'd like to do the same. "There's a category for children," he told him. Seven-year-old Randy looked up at his dad, wide-eyed. "We could show that little calf you like. I'll teach you how to groom her. She's pretty gentle and all you have to do is slowly walk her around the ring. Would you like to do it?" Randy said yes eagerly, excited at the idea.

"It's not hard, but you have to be patient," Brownie explained. "She might get a bit scared, so we'll spend a lot of time with her. She has to get used to you and trust you and learn what she's supposed to do." And for weeks before the fall fair, over and over again, father and son practiced what Randy and his calf would do in the show ring until Randy felt like he could do it in his sleep.

That particular fall fair day was cloudy and threatening to rain as Sheila stood outside the show ring with the other spectators, tightly holding little Simonne's hand, nervously waiting for Randy to come on with his pretty Jersey calf. Behind the gate, Brownie steadied the two young contestants until it was their turn. "*Next Up: Randy Eccles,*" boomed the announcer's voice over the loudspeaker, and Randy, his dark hair slicked into place and his shirt neatly pressed, stepped out into the ring.

"You just have to do it like we've been doing at home," Brownie called out to him as the gate shut behind the pair. Randy nodded, unable to speak for his fear. Very serious and focused, he carefully walked his calf around the show ring for the judging, just as they'd practiced over and over again in the barnyard. It went pretty well for the first few minutes, until the calf realized everyone was looking at her, and decided to stop. Randy gave a tug on the halter, to no effect. He gave another. The calf didn't move. Instead she plopped her clean and carefully brushed body onto the dirt in the ring and sat there. This wasn't something Brownie and Randy had prepared for, but it wasn't the first time Brownie (or the judges) had seen a stubborn calf. It was, however, the first time for Randy, and he didn't know what to do. Despite his best efforts not to cry, when some of the spectators started to laugh, big tears began to roll down his cheeks.

On the sidelines, Sheila gripped Simonne's hand tighter and took a deep breath. Every maternal instinct she had screamed for her to get into that ring and rescue her little boy. "Please, please get up," she urged the calf through gritted teeth, as if that would make it move.

One of the judges, understanding the terror of both the boy and the calf, came down from his seat and yanked the calf to its feet. "Don't cry," he said kindly as he patted Randy on the shoulder. The competition now lost, Brownie joined him, put his arm around Randy, and escorted him and his calf back to the pens. "It's okay," he told Randy gently. "Everyone sometimes has a show day like this. You did well to try. It's not your fault." Randy buried his head in the familiar safety of Brownie's chest and said nothing.

Agnes wasn't the only one who was cheering on Sheila and Brownie's country life from the sidelines, and there were a lot of visitors to the farm in the early 1950s. For those living in New Jersey, Connecticut, and near New York City, it was only a day's drive, or a train trip straight to Palmerston. It was a far cry from their lives in the congestion of the city and the visits provided a chance to feel they were getting a taste of rural life.

Sheila's nephew Tony spent two summers of his teenage years learning to milk cows and throw hay bales. Sheila's sister Kathleen came with her husband Bob and children, and her brother Kevin brought his vivacious wife Marjorie. Sheila's brothers Bernard and Patrick came several times. On his first visit to the farm, Bernard introduced himself to young Randy and Simonne. "Hello, I'm your wicked Uncle Bernard," he said very seriously, looking down from his full height at the children who gawked at him in open-mouthed amazement. Sheila laughed out loud. "Oh, he's just being silly," she told them. However, when Patrick came to visit he had everyone in giggles as he enthusiastically belted out the recently popular song "Walking my Baby Back Home" and pranced Simonne's little dolly carriage around the big kitchen.

For parts of several summers, the old farmhouse was filled with O'Carrolls, everyone chipping in to do chores inside and out, taking turns with the dirty jobs as part of their farm experience. When Sheila needed to call them in from the barn, she stood on the back stoop, took a deep breath, put two fingers in her mouth, and blasted out a long, shrill whistle, a childhood skill she'd learned from her older brothers.

No one expected fancy furnishings or gourmet meals in the farmhouse. They were happy to talk and laugh and share stories of life at 122 Richmond Street. when they had been kids, and as always they argued about politics and philosophy and daily events. *Things are just like they were in Coventry*, Brownie remembered as he leaned back against the kitchen cupboard and took Sheila and her siblings in. "Hey Brownie," Patrick called to him mid-argument about something recently in the news, "are you going to give us your opinion on that story?"

"I would if I could get a word in edgewise," he quipped. They all liked and admired Sheila's quiet farmer, and Brownie enjoyed their company and appreciated their help. Above all, he loved to see his Sheila laughing and relaxed and letting her worries slip away for a bit in the company of her siblings. She was more like the happy-go-lucky girl he'd fallen in love with.

When Sheila's brothers and sisters arrived, happy voices and gales of laughter filled the house. Without them, most of the long days in the farm-house and the barn were quiet ones. The hard work and worries continued, showing in Sheila and Brownie's tired faces and gaunt bodies, until it became increasingly clear that Brownie was not just tired from hard work, but ill too. The most recent letter from Agnes after her annual summer trip to the farm confirmed this to Sheila.

I am very concerned about Brownie and worried about him all the way home. In fact, I just hated to leave you while he had such a high temperature. It is really quite serious for a grown man to have such a high temperature over any length of time. He will need plenty of good nourishing food to build up his resistance again, and in order to prevent any relapse you must see that he gets plenty of rest and sleep. So it is up to you now to put the pounds back on Brownie and tell him not to worry too much. It's a great gamble to get a farm on its feet and the worry of that no doubt helped to lower his resistance. Ask the doctor if he thinks Brownie should have vitamins; that jumpiness you speak of may be indicative of vitamin deficiency.

Sheila read Agnes's letter with growing concern. She knew more sleep for either of them was not an option. They had a farm to run. How could they stop worrying?

As Brownie's poor health dragged on for several more weeks, his doctor finally diagnosed a mild case of polio. Polio epidemics had hit Canada in waves from the 1920s to the early 1950s before a vaccine was introduced. Its symptoms include fever, sore throat, headache, and fatigue, all of which Brownie had. Never quite ill enough to be hospitalized, Brownie just stoically kept going as he always did. Sheila was not the only one who believed in carrying on with a stiff upper lip.

On a dreary November afternoon in 1952, Sheila sat in her kitchen in between her household chores, taking a break to read the latest letter from her old school friend Mary Greenaway. Sheila was weary and worried about the bills as usual, and as she began to read Mary's superficial and silly comments she could almost hear her snooty, self-absorbed voice.

I really was pleased to receive your letter. I'd practically written you off as a dead loss! Busy as you are, I do hope that now you will find time to write more often to me. Sheila please forgive me if I say I was positively staggered at the domestic tone of your letter. I enjoyed reading about your life in Canada. I'm mighty curious about places elsewhere and one gets such conflicting reports about life abroad. Please do tell me what you actually do on the farm Sheila. Do you milk cows? And have you any horses?

Sheila mumbled to herself as she came to the end of the letter. *My life abroad riding my horses!? What do I actually do!?* She looked out the kitchen window over the bare and brown autumn fields. *Mary, Mary, if only you could see me here. My life is such a far cry from what you think it is.* The letter was a vivid reminder of how ill informed Sheila too had once been about the life of a Canadian farm wife. With a sigh, she threw it into a drawer. It would be a long time before it was answered.

It was early January 1953 when Sheila received more bad news. The telegram from Coventry was simple and blunt. *Dad has passed away.* William O'Carroll had died of heart failure peacefully in his sleep, almost seven years since the day she had waved goodbye to him in Liverpool from the top of the double-decker bus, seven years since she'd seen his face or heard the Irish lilt in his voice.

That cold winter night, Brownie left Sheila with the children in the farmhouse to go to see his parents up home for a few hours, as he often did. "I'll stay with you if you like," he offered, already knowing the answer. "No, I want to be alone. Go." Sheila was heartbroken that the little bit of hope she had once had of seeing her father again was now gone forever. She wanted privacy to be with her own thoughts and memories and her pain, but an hour later, when the old crank phone chirped out its distinctive party line ring, she picked it up. No one said hello, and there was no voice except for the sound of someone breathing. "Dad? Dad?" she said, but no one answered, and after a moment the line went dead.

Sheila was too pragmatic to believe in ghosts, but when she recounted this experience in the years to come, she always insisted, "I don't care if you believe me. I know it was my dad. I could feel him. He was calling to tell me goodbye."

For years the O'Carroll siblings in the USA had been trying to convince their parents to immigrate to America. Almost half the family was in the USA or Canada and they believed Nellie and William could have a far better life than struggling in post-war England. Agnes had offered to sponsor them and provide whatever financial support was needed. Despite her pleading, William and Nellie had always resisted, afraid to risk such a huge upheaval in their late years and poor health, but as soon as William died, Agnes increased the pressure on Nellie, now alone and disabled. In all her letters, Agnes had insisted to Sheila and Brownie that the best place for Nellie was in Canada on the farm with them, despite its rural limitations. As soon as they agreed, Agnes wrote to praise them.

I think it is so wonderful of you and Brownie to decide you would like to have her. You have more room than the others and she would be far more comfortable with you. The biggest obstacle is Mother herself. She has her dream about going to America, but it seems she's afraid to make it come real.

It's not going to be as easy as she assumes, Sheila thought as she read Agnes's note. *Mother needs a lot of care every day. I'm thankful I have Brownie's support.*

Finally, in the spring of 1953, just a few months after William had died, bereaved and frail with arthritis, Nellie gave in, with conditions. She agreed to come for a long visit, but drew the line at committing to a permanent move. Nellie had stood up to her bullying father and to an ill-informed doctor when little Sheila had rickets, and had weathered multiple challenges in her life through two world wars and a depression. She was not about to allow her grown children to tell her how or where to live what was left of her life.

"Your English grandmamma is coming!" Sheila sang out to Randy and Simonne in the weeks leading up to Nellie's arrival, her excitement and happiness infectious. She hadn't seen her mother since February 1946, waving goodbye on the doorstep at 122 Richmond Street as Sheila and her dad left for the ship in Liverpool. It was an overdue reunion, bittersweet with William's absence.

By the time Nellie arrived at the farm after her long trip, it was very late on a May evening and the children were in bed. The next morning Sheila took them both by the hand and quietly led them into their former playroom, now a downstairs bedroom, to meet their tiny grey haired grandmother. She was sitting up in the bed, a shawl around her shoulders and a huge welcoming smile on her face. "Come over here my pets, closer, where I can see you better," Nellie said to Randy and Simonne in a voice that sounded to them exactly the same as Sheila's. "Oh, you're so lovely and grown up," she cooed to Randy. "You look like your grandpapa! And look at those blonde curls!" she said to Simonne. "Reach into the drawer of that bedside table and bring me the bag of licorice allsorts. I brought these from England just for you," Nellie explained holding out the bag, "and if you've been good you may take one for a treat." Randy and Simonne reached shyly into the bag to select the perfect piece. Sheila smiled as she watched a scene she had thought she would never see, a lump in her throat. *How very different*, she thought, *from my own grandfather, who wouldn't give a poor little girl a candy.*

Sheila with her mother Nellie and brother Patrick, on the back stoop of the farmhouse, summer 1953.

Nellie stayed on at the farm the rest of that summer and into the fall. In constant pain, she was confined to her wheelchair or her bed, and never ventured much further than the big kitchen or to sit in the sun on the back stoop. Brownie was the only one she trusted to move her. Strong and gentle, he carried her with the utmost care like a fragile piece of china. "I only want Brownie to help me," she insisted when anyone else tried to assist. Sheila provided for her day-to-day personal needs, helping her wash and dress. It was a way for her to reconnect, emotionally and physically, with her mother. It was a chance for the children to know the grandmother they had only heard about in stories and who until then had felt like a character in a book.

"You're a little chatterbox," Nellie said frequently to Simonne. "You're just like my little Sheila."

In the autumn of 1953, Nellie decided it was time to move on to spend some time with her other children in the States. Despite all Agnes's scheming, she never emigrated. It was too much of a leap for her, and she wanted to live what was left of her life in her own home. She had achieved her lifelong goal of seeing her children in America, and she returned to England later that year. She died shortly after.

Sheila wouldn't go back to England for her mother's funeral despite Brownie's encouragement. "We can borrow the money for your airfare," he urged. "You should go."

"What's the point of more debt?" she snapped bitterly. "It won't bring her back. I've already said my good-byes."

The deaths of both her parents, so close together, severed yet another tie to England.

It wasn't long after, as Brownie's health had improved and the farm was beginning to prosper, that a final disaster struck. Before the end of 1954, the Jersey herd Brownie had so carefully planned, bred, nurtured, and loved, was gone, a victim of Bang's disease.

Brownie recognized the first signs of the disease in his cows in the spring. He never knew if it came from an infected animal in the breeding program or was already present in an animal he bought. It may have come from something else altogether. It didn't really matter—the results were the same.

Also known as brucellosis, Bang's is an animal disease related to the birthing process and can affect humans as a bacterial infection, requiring long-term medication. Notably, it can be passed through unpasteurized milk, just as Sheila had insisted. There is no effective treatment for cattle, and as a result, Canada had introduced an eradication program in the 1940s which required the slaughter of all infected and exposed animals.

The day the old veterinarian came to the farm, Brownie hoped against hope he would give a different diagnosis and tell Brownie his suspicions were wrong. "I'm sorry," the vet said as he pulled himself up on creaky knees from examining a cow. His eyes met Brownie's. "There's nothing you can do," he said sadly. "There is no treatment. You know I'm required by law to have you destroy these animals," he said. "All of them," he added after a moment. "They've all been exposed." Brownie could only nod. He knew if he tried to speak, he'd likely cry. The doctor patted Brownie's shoulder gently. "I'll call someone I know to do it, and I'll be here to supervise. We have to get this terrible business done right away."

Silently, Brownie watched the vet pack up his medical bag, turn away and walk out of the barn. He stood motionless for a few minutes with his innocent animals while the bottom fell out of his world, and then slowly closed the barn door, and trudged back to the farmhouse to share the bad news with Sheila.

The process moved quickly. Brownie had killed animals before, as all farmers have to, but this was not something he could do himself. He had an intimate attachment to his cows, had helped them birth calves, had gently touched and talked to them as he collected their milk. His plans of successful farming rested on their warm brown backs. Within days of the visit from the veterinarian, Brownie led his herd of Jerseys to a back field where a bulldozer had already dug a deep trench for the bodies. He stood silently on the sidelines while a hired company shot them one by one and then pushed the bodies into the hole, along with his dreams. His heart was broken. Sheila kept the children in the farmhouse and did not witness the slaughter.

After six years of hard work, sacrifice, ill health, worry, and financial risk, and just as there looked to be a light at the end of the tunnel, it was over within a few days. Brownie was half willing to go further into debt and begin again, but Sheila definitely was not. As far as she was concerned, there would be no more farming. "It's done," she told him firmly the day after the cows were buried. "We have two children to worry about. We'll pay our bills and move forward." Brownie knew she was right, but deep inside he'd hoped she might agree. Head in hands, he finally allowed himself to cry.

The farm sold quickly. An auctioneer was hired for a one-day sale to get rid of the equipment and tools they hoped to sell for enough to cover what was still owing on them. That included the new tractor Brownie had recently purchased to replace his team of draught horses. In dismay, Sheila stood to the side as their possessions were sold off to the highest bidder, their life and tragedy coldly exposed and evaluated, just as they had purchased from other auctions. "That price is too low!" she hissed many times to Brownie throughout the day, hands clenched at her sides. "We still owe more on that." There was nothing he could do. Sheila went to bed that night exhausted and bitter that others had benefitted from their misfortune.

When it was all over, Sheila and Brownie had made enough to settle their farm debts and were left with a small amount for a down payment on their next house. The day they went to town to sign off the final papers, they came back with a new suit for Brownie and a couple of dresses for Sheila, the first new clothes they'd had in years. It was the start of a tradition whenever they sold a house. For the next several decades, it was the only time they ever treated themselves.

CHAPTER 11
THE VILLAGE YEARS: 1954 TO 1963

The little village of Rothsay was well past its prime and might have seemed a strange choice for a fresh start.

A century or so earlier, Rothsay had been a thriving community, but by the mid-1950s it had declined significantly. What remained were about 100 inhabitants, two general stores, a garage/gas station/post office, and a well-used United Church. A number of houses were empty and abandoned, including what was once a hotel on the main street, its long bar still visible through filthy windows. The village was spread over two hills, divided by a busy road and the meandering Conestoga Creek. The one room school, built in 1885, had less than fifteen students in grades one to eight. The small Women's Institute hall saw most of its use as a venue for farewell presentations when a family moved away. It was a measure of the steady erosion of the place.

Here Sheila and Brownie found their new home. There may have been better houses in the bigger towns of Palmerston or Mount Forest, but Brownie had no desire to live anywhere that was even vaguely urban. When they found the Rothsay house and its small acreage for sale, it just felt right. It fit their budget with the little bit of capital they had left after the sale of the farm and its inventory. To Sheila, Rothsay was a bit like an old English village. She was looking forward to being less isolated with other young families nearby.

In distance, it was only a few miles from their former farm. In terms of life circumstances, it proved to be a big leap.

It was raining hard the evening of their first look at the house for sale. A rather pretty storey-and-a-half red brick house with big maple trees in the front, it was located on Head Street, set back a block from the main road, and beside a small playground. The owner, Mr. Williams, had done nothing to update it in the many years he had lived there, but both Sheila and Brownie immediately saw its possibilities, despite the dark night. They knew they needed to go back in the daytime, but for all intents and purposes, they had already made up their minds after that first viewing.

"Brownie, the first thing you need to do is install a septic system. I'm jolly well not going to live in another house without an indoor toilet," Sheila said in the car as they left. "It's 1954 after all! I bet nobody else in the village has an outhouse."

Brownie nodded. "If Mr. Williams accepts our offer, we'll have enough to meet the down payment and make some improvements. I can do most of the work myself. I have some ideas for that little barn at the end of the driveway and we can put a big vegetable garden beside it."

"And we have to paint and get some new linoleum," Sheila added as their excitement grew along with the to-do list. "Did you notice the Loyal Orange Lodge right beside the house?" she asked Brownie, laughing. "It looks like it's not used any more, which is a good thing. My Irish Catholic dad would roll over in his grave if he knew I lived next door to an Orange Lodge of all places!" Brownie just smiled at her concern about an ages-old religious division.

When the papers were finally signed and the house was theirs, they both went to work on the improvements. Sheila squeezed their budget in order to have every room repainted and wallpapered before they moved in. "Look!" she said, taking little Simonne by the hand when they went to inspect the progress of the renovations. They stepped around the painters, their paint cans, and the trestle tables laden with wallpaper and glue. "This will be your bedroom. See all the pink kittens on the walls?" Simonne stood open-mouthed, turning in a circle in the little room, taking it all in.

"Now come here and look at Randy's room. Isn't it wonderful?" Sheila smiled. "See the Mounties and horses on his wallpaper!" Awestruck, Simonne reached out her hand and carefully touched the still damp walls.

In the kitchen cheerful green vines climbed up the wallpaper above the waist-high wainscoting that ran around the big room. It was thoroughly charming.

On the surface, 1950s Rothsay was the kind of community found in wholesome TV shows. There were several families with lots of baby boom kids, although it wasn't called the baby boom until later. The Kirks, the Smiths, the Byes, the McClenaghans, and the Brydons bought their groceries in one or both of the village's general stores, and filled their cars at the village gas pump. They all attended St. James United Church. The children walked to school together and played in the streets as free-range kids did then. The moms were all at home because a married woman wasn't supposed to go out to work unless she was a teacher or a nurse. A working wife was a poor reflection on her husband's ability to support his family. A woman's job was to stay home and raise the children, a responsibility Sheila embraced wholeheartedly.

Randy was a quiet, serious eight-year-old, and Simonne an adventurous and curious four when they moved to Rothsay. Up to this point in her life, Simonne had known nothing but the freedom of a big farm yard to play in, but she was soon to learn that in a village she couldn't wander unrestricted, at least not for a few more years.

Immediately on their arrival in Rothsay, Randy started attending the local school, but Simonne, still too young to go with him, had to stay home. That was okay with her, as she had a lot of exploring to do in her new surroundings, and she constantly badgered Sheila with questions and observations. "Look Mommy, see how the water goes around in the toilet!" she exclaimed, flushing it for the fourth time. "Why does this stair make a funny noise when you jump on it?" Sheila, busy unpacking and sorting out the house, grew tired of Simonne's incessant interruptions and chatter, and sent her to play outside so she could work undistracted for at least a bit. "You must stay in the backyard where I can see you. There's a good girl," Sheila told her. It didn't take long, though, for the curious little explorer to wander to the front yard, dragging a stick along behind her, and to quickly become entranced by the cracks in the sidewalk along Head Street. She was not used to sidewalks. She continued along, exploring block by sidewalk block, crack by crack, until she found herself at the main street, where she stopped to watch the cars and trucks going by. Meanwhile, Sheila, stepping out the back door to call Simonne, found her missing and started to run to find her. Interrupted in the middle of her work, she was disheveled, dressed in a dusty apron and a ragged sweater and her hair hanging askew out of the kerchief around her head, but she didn't care. She was angry and, above all, worried.

"See-mon, See-mon," she called frantically with no response as she ran down the street, finally spying her four-year-old daughter standing at the side of the highway. Relieved, disaster averted, she grabbed Simonne's exploring stick and her arm, turned her around and pointed her in the direction of their new house. "GET. HOME, you wicked girl," she said through gritted teeth, smacking Simonne's little bottom with the stick all the way back, oblivious to her child's humiliated howling and the stares and grins of new neighbours through their windows. It was their first glimpse of the new English woman in town, but not the last impression she was to make.

Down the street from Sheila and Brownie's house, their older neighbor Harmon Mitchell had a small hobby farm, his fields edging one side of the village and his large house with its manicured lawns and pretty flower beds across the street. Sheila hadn't yet met Mrs. Mitchell, but had seen her from a distance and was a bit in awe of the well-dressed teacher. Harmon's cows were kept in the barn across the road from his nice house, but they had a habit of getting through his poorly maintained fences and wandering up to

Brownie's overgrown orchard and from there to Sheila and Brownie's lawn. Perhaps this was acceptable when Mr. Williams lived in the house, but Sheila was having none of it. Oddly, the cows didn't trample through Harmon's well-tended flowerbeds or his lawn, perhaps because, like Sheila, they too respected Mrs. Mitchell.

"Brownie, you have to talk to Harmon about the cows!" Sheila said in exasperation. "I phoned last week and asked him politely to keep them penned but he's done nothing, and there they are again wandering through our property!"

Brownie just shrugged. "There's not much you can do to keep cows fenced if they really want to get out. You know that Sheila."

"That's not good enough! Do something! Talk to him man to man. Soon!" Sheila was at her wits' end. This was worse than being on her own farm with her own cows. At least there she had some control.

Only a few days later, Sheila found another fresh cow patty deposited on the lawn just as she sent Simonne out to play. "Careful! Don't step there!" she warned her. "I've had enough! That's it!" she said with a sigh to no one in particular as she scooped up the still warm and steaming mess on a shovel. "If Brownie can't fix this, I will." Marching it down the street she dropped the load unceremoniously on the front step of Mrs. Mitchell's lovely house. She didn't knock on the door or leave a note.

"I can't believe you did that Sheila," Brownie moaned later that day when she told him, shaking his head in horror and embarrassment for both of them. "I told you I was going to talk to him. Why couldn't you wait?"

Sheila never knew if Mrs. Mitchell stepped in the cow poop in her nice shoes, or perhaps Harmon had removed it before she returned from teaching, but the result was a quick and permanent fixing of the fence. The cows thereafter remained on their own side, and the incident was never spoken of with the Mitchells, although it was no doubt the source of village gossip for a few weeks.

It was sometime later, in the fall of 1955, when Brownie came home with some local news and a suggestion. "Sheila, I heard that the township's looking for a school janitor. The regular caretaker is off sick for a few months and they need someone to fill in. I thought you'd like to do this. It's just a few hours each afternoon when school's over and you can take Simonne with you."

"I have enough to do here," Sheila protested, "and I don't want to be a janitor!" She knew it was a chance to earn a few extra dollars, and that was appealing, but there was a part of her that saw the job as beneath her. "It's just for a while," Brownie urged. "Why not?" Sheila couldn't explain, or admit, why she thought she could do better than cleaning school toilets, and she was disappointed that Brownie had even suggested this job.

But later, swallowing her pride and her reticence, she agreed. "I know we could use the money, so I'll do it—but just for the short term," she said, unenthusiastically. "I'll do my part." After all, how difficult could it be?

The one-room schoolhouse had not changed much since it was built in 1885. It still had rows of Victorian wood and metal desks bolted down to worn wooden floor boards. It was heated with a very old oil-burning space heater at the back of the room. There was no running water and the students and teacher still had to use the deep pit toilets in the cloakroom. The smell was not pleasant at any time, but particularly not in the warmer months. Drinking water was fetched in a pail from the house next door, and from there served in paper cones. Sometimes the students skipped the cones if they were in a hurry and drank straight out of the communal dipper. There was a huge wooden door at the entrance to the school, much too heavy and stiff for the younger children to open without help, and a smaller exit door at the far end of the classroom behind the teacher's desk. That back door was kept permanently locked with a broken bolt, and it continually iced up in winter. No one could use it. In a word, the schoolhouse was a firetrap.

Sheila was appalled at the poor sanitary and safety conditions of the school she was now seeing up close every day. It was worse than she'd thought. A year earlier she had encountered the same archaic situation in the one-room school Randy had attended near the farm, but she had expected something better in the village. Very quickly she made a list of the most glaring issues and brought her concerns to the attention of the three school board trustees.

"Did you know there's no second exit for the students in case of fire?" she told each one in separate phone calls. "If that old stove blows up, there's no way to get past it to the front door and the back door won't open! How will they get out?" Only one of the three trustees paid any attention. He shared her worries and had even told his own children not to drink the water at the school, not trusting its quality. No one else seemed interested in health and safety, or more to the point, spending the money it would cost to make improvements. The elected trustees were older men who had been on the board for a long time and were annoyed at this pushy young English woman.

Sheila pointed out that they needed a reliable water source and sanitary toilets. She noted the only fire extinguisher was not operational and no fire drills were ever held. "Could you please replace the back door?" she pleaded again and again. "Or at least install a new lock so it can be opened in case of a fire."

"Mrs. Eccles, those repairs are expensive and we don't have that kind of money in the budget."

"Mrs. Eccles, you'll be gone in a few months. Your job's only temporary, so don't worry about it."

"Mrs. Eccles, every other school in the township is the same. It's been good enough up to now. The other caretaker never said anything about it. "

Sheila's suggestions were ignored. As she cleaned the school every day she grew angrier and more frustrated, worrying about Randy and the other children at risk, with Simonne about to join them soon.

The annual meeting of the school board was held on a winter night in December 1955 in the old school house. The building was hot in more ways than one; it was packed with more attendees than usual, and the local residents sensed a confrontation and some excitement. Word had gotten around. They were perched on the wooden desks, sweating in their heavy winter coats, watching the three trustees at the front of the room go through their agenda. The sole trustee who agreed with Sheila stood up and listed the safety issues, making a motion to fund the repairs. As he tried to add his own concerns about some questionable financial practices in the annual statement of the board, he was interrupted by derision from the other trustees and loud heckling from the crowd. Anyone else brave enough to speak up about the needed improvements was shouted down, including Sheila and Brownie. It was an unruly and threatening demonstration.

Shocked by the behavior at the public meeting, and faced with the continued indifference of the elected school board, Sheila decided to take the matter into her own hands. "Brownie, let's just fix that back door ourselves. I'll bet you have some kind of lock in all your hardware bits and pieces in the shed. Can you install it?" she asked. Brownie nodded his agreement. "I'll do it this weekend," he said. "They might not even notice and they sure won't say thank you, but it needs to be done."

With or without permission Sheila was determined to move ahead to repair the unsafe oil stove as well, and phoned an oil burner mechanic in Palmerston to see what he could do. She arranged to talk to him when she went to town to replace the old fire extinguisher, again at her own cost. What Sheila didn't know, however, was that someone was listening in to her party line phone conversations, and knew her plans. As she was driving into Palmerston later that day, one of the opposing trustees sped past her and pulled into the hardware store just ahead of her. "Go home Mrs. Eccles," he sneered as she stepped out of her car. "You're not needed here." The new fire extinguisher was installed that week.

On New Year's Day, 1956, Sheila wrote a letter to the editor of the *Palmerston Observer*, decrying the behavior of what she called "the mob" at the school board meeting of a week or so earlier. *To witness a long line of approximately twenty men leer, sneer, and jeer, and crowd threateningly towards one individual* (the dissenting trustee) *reeks sadly of shades of secret police states and cannot be tolerated in a democratic country like Canada.*

It is no wonder our teenagers revert to the law of the jungle when they see this example from their elders.

It had not been long since she and Brownie had seen firsthand the damage done in Europe by organized Nazi bullies, and Sheila was keenly aware of the harm that could be done. She'd heard her father talk about the confrontations and violence of political groups in Ireland, but hadn't expected to find such similar behaviour in peaceful and quiet Canada.

Sheila's letter was picked up by the bigger *Kitchener-Waterloo Record*, and a few months later, in April of 1956 they wrote an exposé of the local school board. By then Sheila's term as janitor was long over and the sole supportive trustee had lost his seat. The reporter described her as a modest woman who didn't want to take credit for the improvements. In typical 1950s style, her first name wasn't even included in the story. She was Mrs. WJB Eccles, not Sheila. Her identity was that of her husband. It was the way it had always been for married women.

One year later, running water and flush toilets were installed in the school, the furnace was replaced, and fire drills were routine.

Sheila caused a big kerfuffle in the little community, and for sure there were some hard feelings about the stubborn English woman who tried to tell them what to do. It was to be one of Sheila's first steps on the road to initiating small social changes. It would not be her last.

Sheila and Brownie's home in Rothsay

CHAPTER 12
THE DOMESTIC YEARS:
1950's

Sheila was thirty-five years old when she moved to Rothsay. Well spoken and well read, with a lot of life experience under her belt, she'd seen a bit of the world, at least more than most of the women she knew. She'd gone from being a carefree bank teller to a soldier and a farmer, and now in her prime was a rural housewife and mother of two children. While she embraced her domestic role and loved her family, she tried to ignore the niggling voice at the back of her brain telling her she could do better. She felt she could reach higher, but how? Ten years earlier, when she thought the future held unlimited possibilities, she hadn't counted on endless loads of laundry and "women's work."

Financial security always seemed to be out of reach. Despite Brownie's hard work and Sheila's frugal management, there was just never enough money, and Sheila relentlessly urged and nagged Brownie to better his situation. Her wellbeing, and her children's, was totally dependent on Brownie's earning power. It would be frowned on in the 50s if she were to contribute to the family's finances with her own paycheque, so she channeled her efforts into improving Brownie's prospects.

Brownie's lack of education was one of the stumbling blocks to better employment, and while Sheila correctly identified this, she specifically focused on Brownie's poor grammar. In England, how one spoke was a clear measurement of social level, and one could not get ahead with imperfect language. Thus, Sheila rarely missed an opportunity to correct her husband.

"I seen the Smiths in the store today," Brownie started to tell her.

"I saw," Sheila interrupted automatically, without taking her eyes away from what she was doing at the kitchen sink. "Go on."

"I saw," he repeated quietly. Or, biting his tongue, he didn't reply at all.

Poor grammar grated on her like fingernails on a blackboard, and her responses were so reflexive she often corrected him regardless of who might overhear.

It wasn't just Brownie's grammar that challenged Sheila. Her objective was more than the purely selfish goal of ensuring a higher income. She saw it as her responsibility to try to help him achieve his potential. Like most other farmers of his generation, Brownie had never gone to high school, and for years Sheila pushed him to take night courses to achieve at least a grade ten. That educational milestone would open doors to many more job opportunities.

"I see in the newspaper that the Board of Education night classes are scheduled to start again. Why don't you sign up for the upgrading program?" Sheila urged. "I can get you the application form tomorrow." Brownie ignored her. He was an easy-going man who generally avoided confrontations, but here he dug in his heels and refused to be bullied. And as stubbornly, Sheila remained tenacious in her efforts to create a new and improved version of the man she had found so irresistible in 1945.

A generation later, when Simonne announced she was getting married, Sheila's only advice was cryptic. "Don't go into this thinking you'll change him. It doesn't work."

The post-war economy in the early 50s was hard on young couples in Canada, but times were even tougher for those back in England. As Sheila and Brownie were settling into life in Rothsay trying to pick up the pieces after the failure of the farm, Sheila's sister Tess and her husband Joe and two kids were planning to leave Coventry and come to Canada, as Sheila had been urging them to do for some time. There were few jobs, limited housing, and continuing food shortages in England. Tess and Joe had shared the little house at 122 Richmond Street with Sheila's parents and helped to care for them before they died, but once they were gone there was little reason to stay on. Their hard decision to emigrate was made.

"Your Auntie Tess is coming!" Sheila sang repeatedly to Randy and Simonne in the weeks ahead of their arrival, bustling excitedly to make preparations. "And so are your cousins Ruth and Michael, who are almost the same ages as you. It's going to be ever so lovely," she said as she readied the little guest room. Sheila was thrilled that someone from her own family would soon be nearby to share old O'Carroll traditions, a sister who would understand her funny English ways.

Tess and Joe and their two young children arrived on a dark, cold evening in early 1955 and squeezed into the spare bedroom with all their belongings. The house was magically filled with chatter and activity. "I'll put the kettle on and let's have a proper English cup of tea," Sheila said as they all crowded around the kitchen table. "You must be exhausted. I know what that trip feels like."

"It's bloody good of you to have us, Brownie," Joe said. The brothers-in-law had met on only a couple of occasions ten years earlier, before Brownie returned to Canada. Essentially, they were almost strangers. "You know you're welcome here, and I'll keep my ears open for any jobs," Brownie replied. For Tess, Joe, and the children, everything seemed quite unlike what they'd left behind, and clearly it was different from their expectations. Coming from urban Coventry, bustling even with its heavy bomb damage, to the isolation and snow of a tiny rural Ontario village was a shock.

"Is there a pub nearby?" Joe asked, hoping for an outing for them all and maybe a chance to meet some villagers. "Oh no," Brownie laughed. "In Ontario only men go to a bar, and children definitely aren't allowed."

"It's not like at home," Sheila added. "People here are shocked if you suggest a family meal where there's alcohol. They don't have real pubs like we do." There were no buses, no theatres, and not even a restaurant in Rothsay. A car was needed to get to the closest doctor or pharmacy.

"Where's the Catholic Church?" Tess asked. "We'll have to drive you to Arthur," Sheila replied, a bit ashamed to admit to her sister that she no longer attended. "I go to the United Church next door now with Brownie." Even the neighbours were mostly unseen, staying in their warm houses except for shoveling snow. Much like Sheila's arrival at the old family farmhouse ten years earlier, coming to Canada jolted Tess and Joe.

It didn't take long before Joe was hired as a prison guard at the reformatory in Guelph. It was not the job he had hoped for in Canada, but it was a start at setting up their own home. With the loan of some furniture from Brownie and Sheila, the family was able to get settled in a Guelph apartment, half an hour's drive from Rothsay. Neither of them having a car, it was too far for Sheila and Tess to see each other often, and phone calls in the mid-1950s were expensive, so their chats became more infrequent. Even though Guelph was a much bigger town with many more amenities, with Joe working shift work, there were many long and lonely days for Tess as she tried to adjust to a new life in Ontario and settle her kids into a domestic routine quite unlike what they came from. Sheila was happy to have one of her siblings nearby, but she worried about her far less outgoing younger sister and how she was adapting. It turned out she wasn't coping very well at all.

"There's no school uniforms here!" Tess complained to Sheila during a visit. "The children have to wear their own clothes." Sheila had been surprised at that too. "And why do people look at me strangely when I use words like jumper instead of sweater?"

"You'll get used to it," Sheila assured her. "After a while it doesn't matter. People still correct me when I say *bluebreeze* instead of blue berries. Don't worry about it. Just smile at them and keep your chin up."

"And I can't find decent proper English biscuits," Tess moaned. "And the tea's not even the same!

"It's easier for you, though," Tess added. "You have a Canadian husband." Sheila knew exactly how her sister felt, but she said to herself, *Best not to encourage her dissatisfaction.*

Unbeknownst to Sheila, Tess had secretly begun to squirrel away every cent she could to return to England. Everything was so different and strange to her in Canada. Her challenges were as simple as how words were accented and as complex as social interactions. The pronunciation of words like walk and talk grated on her. More importantly, it was very difficult for shy Tess to make new friends. Her isolation was compounded by Joe's shift work. Her children were at school and she was alone a lot, desperately homesick for the life she had left behind. The hardships she had experienced in England now seemed much less significant compared to her life in Canada. Sheila had experienced all the same frustrations and resentments and homesickness, but had weathered them on her own.

Sheila was far more adventurous than Tess, didn't recognize the signals Tess was sending, was convinced she would feel better over time. Sheila was busy with her own family responsibilities and the challenges of the school safety issues. In truth, she didn't really know her younger sister all that well. Sometimes a couple of weeks would go by without the sisters speaking.

Then, one day when Sheila walked to the little post office in Rothsay to pick up the mail, there was a letter postmarked England. It was from Tess. Without a word of warning, she and Joe had packed up and left Canada only about a year after arriving. They sold the household furnishings Sheila and Brownie had lent them to help pay for their tickets. There was no in-person goodbye or even a telephone call, and very little explanation in the letter.

Sheila sat speechless at the kitchen table, the letter in her hand, sad, confused, and very hurt. "Oh Brownie, I've had a letter from Tess," she said to him as soon as he came through the door from work later that day. "They've gone back to Coventry! Without a word!"

"What? Why did they leave?" he asked, stunned. "When did this happen?"

" I don't know, do I? If I had known, I would have talked to her!" Sheila answered, her voice breaking. "What did I do wrong? Didn't we help enough?"

"I think we helped lots," Brownie assured her, a hand on her shoulder. "That wasn't the problem. Tess isn't strong like you. You did everything you could."

As the finality of Tess's decision sunk in, Sheila went through the motions of that evening in a fog. She put Randy and Simonne to bed, and much later, as she was slipping into bed herself beside Brownie, she whispered, "What will my sisters in the States think of me? They'll figure I'm to blame." Brownie, already asleep, didn't answer.

Sheila was ashamed to explain Tess' retreat to her Canadian in-laws. But mostly, she was devastated to lose the only family member she had had nearby. Her mother Nellie had decided not to stay in Canada, and now Tess had done exactly the same. They had both raised her hopes and then deserted her.

"I just wanted to be with my own people," was the only explanation Tess gave, years later.

It was one more brick in the wall of Sheila's isolation and loneliness. One more reason to feel she could depend on no one but herself. Although they continued to write letters, Sheila and Tess were never again to see each other face to face.

This was the era when waves of eastern European immigrants were arriving in Toronto, and there were often observations around the Sunday dinner table at Brownie's parents' farm about these new Canadians. Many of Brownie's brothers and sisters lived in areas where the new arrivals were moving into, and they joked about the odd ways of these people. "You should see the kind of sausages in the butcher shops these DPs eat! The garlic from them is enough to make your eyes water." They made fun of their accents and strange traditions. Sheila, always sensitive to the challenges of emigration, got angry. She had read in the newspapers about the terrible injustices the immigrants had endured and saw nothing to joke about.

"These are *displaced people*," she bristled, "Don't call them DPs. It's demeaning. They've been forced out of their homes in war torn countries where everything they had was destroyed!" Sheila was never one to back down from an argument, even at her mother-in-law's table. "You have no idea what they've been through," she lectured. Sheila's black eyes flashed and her voice got louder. "You have never been hungry or lost your home or had your family put in a concentration camp." She was remembering the starving people she had witnessed not so many years earlier in Belgium and the Netherlands. Brownie, who had seen just as much wartime destruction, perhaps more, stayed quiet. He didn't want an argument, and just looked on as his brothers joked and cajoled Sheila. They all knew how serious she was about social issues and they wanted to wind her up. "Ah, c'mon Sheila. You know we're just having fun. We really like the new people in the apartment next door and we kid them too. They laugh. Why can't you?"

"Because this is wrong!" she answered, "Even if you're kidding, it's not funny. Just because they are different doesn't make them less. Don't mock them. Help them."

She fully understood what it felt like to be an outsider.

CHAPTER 13
HAPPIER DAYS?
1956

1954 would be remembered for the failure of the farm, and 1955 for Sheila's fight with the school board and the disappointment of her sister's return to England, but 1956 was noteworthy for a much happier event: the arrival of twins.

Sheila, always lean and fit, watched in amazement as her body rapidly expanded in the early winter months of '56. Both of her previous babies had been healthy, large, full-term deliveries, but with the third pregnancy, she felt as if she was becoming as round as she was tall. In the mid-1950s, before much was developed in the way of pre-natal testing, the doctor had concerns about her size and the risks to her health.

"Thirty-seven is old to be having a baby, Mrs. Eccles," he told her, not mincing any words. "Pregnancy is a lot more difficult for someone your age as you know. It's a good thing you're healthy over all and this isn't your first delivery, but you're getting much too big too fast. I can only hear one heart-beat so we can't blame your size on twins. You've got to take it easy."

"How am I supposed to take it easy?" Sheila mumbled to herself as she squeezed her bulk behind the steering wheel of her car to return home. "Easy for the doctor to say."

It was hard to be hugely pregnant in the winter months when Sheila's everyday jobs were largely physical and included keeping the woodstove going and pushing wet sheets and Brownie's work clothes through a wringer washer. It was even harder to carry the heavy laundry basket outside to hang everything on the line in the freezing cold. Brownie did his best to help her when he came home from work each day, and Simonne was recruited to tie her mother's shoes and fetch anything that involved bending over. Nine-year-old Randy's job was to carry in the wood and kindling every day after school to fill the woodbox and to take out the ashes. But even with their help, in the early months of 1956, Sheila became terribly uncomfortable and found it difficult to move around.

"If you fall down outside," Brownie quipped, "you'll start to roll and turn into a huge snowball!" Sheila laughed, despite her fatigue and discomfort. "Please promise me you'll be careful in the ice and snow," he asked. Even the neighbours were concerned enough to keep an eye on Sheila during the day.

The winter weather had hung on that year, and it felt like spring would never come. There was still snow on the ground and the temperature was below freezing on the afternoon of April 15th when Sheila woke from her after lunch nap on the cot in the kitchen. "Simonne, I need you," she called. "You have to go across the street to Mrs. Kirk and tell her it's time." This had been rehearsed over and over again in the weeks leading up to April, and five-year-old Simonne knew precisely what she was supposed to do. "Put your boots on and do up your coat. It's cold out. Do NOT stop to dawdle on your way! I'll be watching from the window. Go now. There's a good girl."

Mrs. Kirk, at home with her own babies, immediately set the plan into action. She phoned the neighbor who was designated to drive Sheila to the hospital in Palmerston, and kept Simonne with her until the driver returned to take her to her own house where they would wait to catch Randy on his way home from school. It was all well choreographed. Everyone was assigned to their roles and eager to fulfill them, and by dinnertime, the entire village was waiting for news.

Early the next morning, April 16th, a tired but elated Brownie arrived at the neighbours' house to wake Simonne and Randy with his news. "We have TWO babies!" he announced, simultaneously beaming and tearful, holding Simonne on his lap and with his arm around Randy. "Two babies! A boy and a girl! There's one for each of you!"

Born half an hour apart, a little after midnight, the twins had a combined weight of more than sixteen pounds. They were named Scott, for Brownie's father, and Holly, just because Sheila liked the name.

Sheila's life had been busy before the twins, but it became far more so when the number of her children doubled. This was long before disposable diapers, and she was faced with mountains of cloth diapers to put through the wringer and hang on the clothesline every day. In the colder months her hands were so dry they cracked and bled. "Ouch, don't touch me," Randy and Simonne complained when Sheila bathed them in the tin bathtub. "Your hands are scratching me!"

On the coldest days, the diapers hung over clothes racks beside the woodstove or on the lines Brownie had strung over the stairwell. In the summer months, the diapers were spread across the lawn to dry on the grass, Sheila's theory being that the chlorophyll would help to kill bacteria.

Before the introduction of pre-made baby formula, she filled dozens of sterilized glass baby bottles with the carefully measured mixture of evaporated milk, water, and corn syrup recommended by the Public Health Unit, lining the bottles up in rows on the kitchen table like an assembly line. All of this was done between nursing and caring for two babies who didn't always sleep at the same time, and keeping up with the needs of her two older children. Her life was far from glamorous.

In the decades before the throw-away economy, Sheila and Brownie wasted nothing. Their generation had been raised in the Depression of the 30s and they knew how to re-use and repair. Brownie could fix almost anything that broke and his big vegetable garden supplied most of their summer needs. The children's clothes were rarely new, but instead were hand-me-downs from older cousins or friends. Even Brownie's heavy wool work socks were darned and re-darned.

One evening before she was to perform at the school's Christmas concert, twelve-year-old Simonne brought her tights to Sheila in dismay. "I need new ones! Look at the big hole in the leg! I can't wear these!

"Don't worry. Give them to me," Sheila said calmly, "I'll try to fix them. It's too late to find any new ones and these will have to do." That night after Simonne had gone to bed, she painstakingly darned them with the closest matching yarn she could find. "This shows! I look stupid!" Simonne cried when she put them on the next morning. "No one will think less of you," Sheila said cheerfully, in response to her daughter's tears. "It's better than a hole, isn't it? That darned knee shows that someone loves you enough to take care of you."

On one occasion when she couldn't afford a new outfit to wear to a family wedding, Sheila pulled her old wartime sandals out of the back of the closet and painted them silver with stove pipe paint. She wore them with a pretty summer dress she'd had since 1945 and could still fit into after four children. "Oh, Sheila, you look so lovely!" admired many of her sisters-in-law.

Most of the time she was not so well attired. When it was very cold and the woodstove and the oil heater couldn't keep the house sufficiently warm, Sheila wore her rubber overshoes inside, with a pair of Brownie's wool socks for extra insulation. If that didn't help, she folded up old newspapers for an extra insole, as she'd done during the war. She wore layers of sweaters, cinched on with one of Brownie's belts. Often, on really cold nights, she got out of her warm bed and, with just her flashlight, went from room to room to spread a heavy winter coat over each child's bed for extra warmth.

Sheila's nocturnal well-being checks continued as long as she had her children in the house. "Thanks Mom," murmured a sleepy teenage Scott on a cold night as he felt Sheila spreading a blanket over him in the dark. "I didn't mean to wake you up. Just thought you might be cold," she whispered as he snuggled back to sleep in the comfort and security of his warm bed and his mother's love.

Meanwhile, the conflicting feelings Sheila felt about her role continued to grow and were getting harder to ignore, a push-pull between her domestic responsibilities and her thoughts that surely there ought to be more to her life than this. Like other women of her generation, in the last half of the 1950s Sheila felt constrained by the responsibilities of raising her kids and the expectations of being a housewife. She was boxed into one role only. It was a far cry from her independent and happy-go-lucky days in the army, but Sheila was determined, most of the time, to make the best of things and carry on. She convinced herself there was adventure and fun to be found in the most mundane things.

On a hot summer afternoon, with pots of water and pickling juice boiling on the stove, Sheila had her sleeves rolled up and a rag around her head to hold back her hair. Sweat was running down her face but she was determined to master the seven-day pickle recipe so popular with her friends. "Stay back. I don't want to spill any of this hot juice on you," she warned her children gathered around the table to watch as she carefully filled jars. The kids were fascinated by the plain old cucumbers from the garden turning into a bright green condiment. They were even more excited when Sheila started to sing her version of a Broadway hit.

All I want is a brand new car, lots of pickles in a big jam jar.
Then I could go oh so far, oh wooouldn't it be loverly!

Grabbing a hand of each of the giggling twins, she twirled and danced them through the house. In those moments, she was *My Fair Lady*'s Liza Doolittle, wishing for better times and belting out her own musical dream with her children as the chorus.

Other summer days in Rothsay passed far more slowly. Sheila found herself restless for something more interesting than her domestic tasks. She wanted to explore—ideas, places, possibilities—and the close-by empty Presbyterian Manse looked like a place to start. Pretending to be just going for a walk, the children trailing behind her like little ducklings, she strolled up the street to the old house. "Where are we going Mom?" asked a twin. "Let's just go for a walk and see what we can find," she urged. She was curious about this lovely, neglected place on the hill with its view over Rothsay and the creek. "Come on. We're just looking. Nothing wrong with that." She brushed the dirt off a windowpane and pressed her nose to the glass to look in. "Oh, how interesting," she said as she gently pushed up the sash of the window. "I wonder if it might open." It did. She climbed through and pulled each child in behind her. "Mom, we're not allowed to be in here!"

"We'll just have a look around. I don't think anyone will mind," she said, as she slowly wandered through and marveled at the big rooms, looking out the bay window at the village beyond. "Look! You've never seen one of these before. This is a dumb waiter!"

"What's that for?" Holly asked. "It's like a little elevator to send food upstairs to the bedrooms," Sheila replied. "Imagine having breakfast in bed!" She showed them how it worked and then they admired the butler's pantry with its built in glass cabinets. "Oh, it's all so lovely! Wouldn't it be wonderful to live here?" She returned to go through the unlocked window a few more times that summer, allowing herself to daydream about the possibility of living in a grand house.

In the long summer stretch of school holidays, afternoon tea was both a diversion and a ritual. "Here you go. Come and have some tea," Sheila called to whatever kids were around. "It's time to sit down and have a rest in the shade. It's true what they say you know," and she sang. *Only mad dogs and Englishmen go out in the mid-day, out in the mid-day, out in the mid-day sun*! While Sheila had real tea, the children had watery Kool-Aid, made special with a plate of English Peek Frean cookies on her favorite metal tray featuring a picture of Queen Elizabeth at her coronation. Occasionally the treat was Sheila's real homemade sugary lemonade. The other mothers might sometimes find a few cents for a popsicle, but the Rothsay kids preferred Sheila's more elegant afternoon events.

Sheila was in the kitchen one August afternoon when she heard the kids urgently calling her. "Mom, quick, get out here! Mom! Don't miss this!"

Rushing out the door to the front lawn, wondering what the excitement was about, she was greeted by the sight of a long line of army vehicles rumbling right past the house. The kids watched in awe. Something like this had never before been seen in Rothsay. It might have been summer cadets on some sort of manoeuvre, but regardless of why they were there on her street, Sheila was suddenly transported back in time and place to her own army convoys, the noise and dust of the big trucks, the smell of the engines, the canvas roofs slapping in the wind. Sheila whipped off her apron and stood stock still like the soldier she used to be, her shoulders back as the vehicles slowly passed by. At the end of the long line of trucks came two open jeeps carrying the officers. As they passed, Sheila crisply snapped her arm up in salute. A little surprised, but clearly pleased, and recognizing her military bearing, the officers returned her salute. The children stared; invisible bystanders dropped into one of the stories their mother had so often told them.

Sheila held her salute until the convoy passed. Only then did she bring her arm down and stand for a moment until they'd turned the corner, and, with a sigh, stoop to pick up her apron and went back into the house.

Sheila never voiced she was unhappy with her life or that she missed her carefree pre-marital days, never shared regrets for opportunities lost, or wished out loud for some adventure. She carefully guarded those feelings like a secret. Her children were loved and well cared for, their imaginations nurtured through her own, and their ambitions, encouraged. But occasionally, despite her stiff upper lip, her discontent and frustration with the constraints of her life poked through.

"Mom, Mom, can you iron my dress?"

"Moooom, why is dinner late? I'm hungry!"

"C'mon Mom, I don't want to do that. Why can't you do it for me?'

When the litany of whining demands and complaints became too much, Sheila snapped. "What would you do if I was *dead*!?" The outburst shocked her children into silence. It was an expression she'd heard from her own mother and one she used many more times over the coming years when she reached her breaking point.

Once, when a much anticipated special event had been cancelled, preteen Simonne was distraught. Sheila was not responsible for the event or for the disappointment, but she became the brunt of Simonne's sulking and complaining. "Stop crying!" Sheila said sharply. "Life is full of disappointments. You might as well get used to it."

At the kitchen table one afternoon, Sheila picked up the recently arrived Sears catalogue to browse through while she had her cup of tea. "Here's a nice coat. Maybe I should order it for next spring," she said wistfully, deep in thought.

"What do you need a new coat for?" piped up one of the kids innocently. "You never go anywhere."

Sheila said nothing for a moment, stunned at the truth of her child's observation. "No," she finally replied sadly. "And I guess I never will."

Confined by domesticity and journeys not much further than the distance between her ironing board and her vacuum cleaner, Sheila nonetheless moved in the world of ideas and facts, gleaned almost entirely from her voracious newspaper reading and listening to the CBC. With no access to a bookstore or library, she rarely read books. If there were words and concepts she didn't know she looked them up in her well-worn one volume encyclopedia and the tattered dictionary she had brought with her from England. It was not unusual for her to sit late at night, after everyone had gone to bed, enjoying a cigarette in the quiet house with her friend the newspaper. There wasn't much she didn't know or hadn't heard about.

"What does *obstreperous* mean Mom?"

"It means noisy, someone who distracts you and gets in the way and is annoying. Like you sometimes when you're a nuisance," she joked.

"Mom, what's the capital of Brazil? I need it to finish this map for geography."

"Brasilia," she answered immediately. "It's a specially designed new city."

"Who's Diefenbaker, Mom?"

"That's John Diefenbaker, the Prime Minister. They call him Dief the Chief. There was an interesting article about him in yesterday's newspaper."

Sheila was Google before it had been invented, but her information didn't always bode well for the family.

There had been numerous sightings of rabid foxes in the vicinity one very cold winter, and they had been known to attack people without warning. Even the CBC was reporting this story, and Sheila heard an expert recommending that people carry a large stick to ward off any attacks from an animal. *What a good idea,* she thought, worrying about Simonne walking the long, isolated road to school, vulnerable to a sick predatory fox. *She needs something to defend herself.* Searching through Brownie's woodpile she found just the right branch, sturdy enough to be effective but not too heavy for Simonne to carry.

"What am I supposed to do with that?" Simonne whined when Sheila handed her the weapon.

"If a fox tries to attack you, you hit it with the stick. See?" Sheila swung it around.

"Everybody's going to laugh at me! I can't walk to school carrying that stupid thing!"

"Don't argue with me. You'll take it with you every day until we hear that the threat is over. Do what you're told."

Mortified, Simonne obediently dragged the stick along with her for weeks, hoping unsuccessfully that no one would notice, but too afraid to defy her mother just in case she was right, as she so often was. The only real threat Simonne encountered was the ridicule of the other kids at school. "Your mother's crazy!".

That same cold winter Sheila fretted about Randy freezing as he waited for the high school bus. "I have just the thing for you!" she announced happily when he came home one afternoon shivering from the icy weather. "Uncle Tom gave us this big fur coat he's had for ages. I think it'll fit you and be perfect for those cold mornings." Randy, forever polite and nonconfrontational like Brownie, shrugged himself into the ugly old overcoat. "Oh, it fits perfectly!" Sheila said. "It goes right to your knees and it'll keep your bottom from freezing."

"I really don't want to wear this," Randy said quietly. "I'll look stupid."

"It's lovely. You look like a Mountie! The other kids'll think it's cool and really fun."

Randy wore it as Sheila knew he would, despite his discomfort. It was heavy and moth eaten in places and looked like it came from the turn of the century. Both Randy and Simonne recognized it was pointless to try to resist or out-argue Sheila in these matters, and so they endured the public humiliation of their English mother's unusual ideas.

Long before the internet and the ability to dispense opinions instantly, Sheila shared her inquiries and ideas the old-fashioned way with handwritten letters. On a summer afternoon, dreaming about how nice it would be to have a much-needed, but highly unlikely, vacation, she wrote a long letter to a lodge on Georgian Bay inquiring about a self-catering stay in a cottage. The manager quickly responded, telling her that mothers need a vacation too and urging her to come. She wouldn't need to cook, all meals were provided, and there was maid service. She could do nothing but sit by the lake and relax. It was a nice dream for a day or two.

One of Sheila's letters went to the Shirriff pudding company. Her favorite dessert was butterscotch or chocolate pudding, made from a mix added to milk and cooked on the stove. Sheila had discovered that putting waxed paper over the pudding as it cooled not only kept any flying bugs out of it, but also had the side effect of preventing a skin from forming on the surface. She wrote to the company to share her tip. A nice reply thanked her and then she heard nothing more. It was not until years later that Sheila's wax paper idea appeared as a suggestion on the side of the pudding box. No credit was ever given.

Hard as it was to reconcile with her sense of adventure and fun, Sheila was a worrier, especially when it came to her kids. It was not just rabid foxes or unpasteurized milk that concerned her. Food poisoning was high on her list, and before there were reliable portable coolers, she was convinced that picnics posed a significant risk.

At the Eccles family reunion one summer, Sheila refused to participate in the traditional meal sharing and insisted that the children eat only what she had packed for the picnic. In her lunch there was no mayonnaise or salad dressing, no butter, and no other foods which she believed might spoil in the heat. "We're going to sit here at our own table so you won't be eating what the others have brought," she told the kids. "It might not be safe."

"But Mom," all four of them protested, "what about the potato salad?"

"I want some devilled eggs!"

"I feel stupid sitting over here by ourselves."

Brownie was embarrassed. "Sheila, we always share. You know that. Sitting over here by ourselves is insulting. What am I supposed to say to everyone?"

"I don't care what you tell them. I don't want my children eating things that might make them sick. If you want to eat with your family, go ahead. It's up to you. We're staying here."

Brownie knew there was no way to change her mind. His sisters and brothers and parents looked over from their long table loaded with cold chicken and potato salad and all the good food he loved. They chuckled and shrugged their shoulders at this latest of Sheila's strange ideas, and went on enjoying their lunch. Sighing, Brownie sauntered over to the big table and sat down. He shook his head and offered little in the way of explanation. After sampling his mother's apple pie, he came back to Sheila and the kids to finish his lunch there. When they had eaten, they packed up and joined the rest of the family and the reunion carried on as it always had. When Sheila wasn't looking, Brownie's sister Ella slipped a couple of butter tarts to each of the kids. "It's not poison," she whispered with a grin.

Sheila had heard a lot of news stories about the perils of lightning hitting a house, even knocking out a staircase and trapping the family upstairs. Thereafter, whenever a big thunderstorm struck, she got all the children out of bed and made them come downstairs. She refused to talk on the phone in a thunderstorm because she had read about someone being electrocuted through a phone line, and she unplugged every appliance and lamp.

She never left a knife on the kitchen counter when she went to bed, in case someone broke in and used it as a convenient weapon to slash her throat.

After the collapse of the snow-covered arena roof in Listowel in February 1959 tragically killed several children, she forbade her kids from going to any arena, for any reason.

Sheila was constantly vigilant regarding her children's well being, occasionally in a bizarre and neurotic way, but she was more often right than wrong. Electrical appliances were known to start fires, raw milk was proven to cause disease, and people did get electrocuted (rarely) by telephones. Her ideas were not as crazy as they sounded at the time. Sometimes it just took years for them to become general knowledge.

But one day in 1959 it was an encounter with a pedophile that really showed just how undaunted Sheila was when it came to protecting her family.

Early summer 1956. Simonne and Randy with newborn twins Scott (left) and Holly (right) in front of the house in Rothsay.

CHAPTER 14
BIG CHANGES:
EARLY 1960's

The ladies at the United Church were doing a summer clean up and had asked Sheila to pitch in. *Why not?* she thought. *It's just next door and I can give them an hour or so while the twins are napping and have a good old chat with the neighbours. Randy'll stay in the house and keep an eye on everything. It'll be fine.*

Simonne was in the backyard where she'd been told to stay, playing a solitary make-believe game when her reverie was suddenly broken. "Hello? Anyone here?" A man was walking up the driveway carrying an empty pail.

"I need some drinking water for the road crew working on the highway. Can I use the pump in your yard?" He pointed to the old hand pump over the fenced-off well.

"We're not supposed to touch that. It's not safe." Simonne was unsure what to do but trying to be helpful. "You can get water from the kitchen tap inside. My mother's not home but I'll call my brother."

"No, wait a minute," he said as she turned towards the house. His attention had moved to the small barn. "What's in there? Show me."

He was already opening the door and moving into the cooler shadows of the building. Simonne, worried what he was doing, followed him. "There's no pump in here. Just daddy's tools and stuff." Something didn't feel right about this but she didn't know what it was.

He turned towards her with a smile. "How much do you weigh? If I pick you up I bet I can tell you." And before Simonne could answer or back away, he reached down and in one movement lifted her up, held her tightly to his body and pressed his open mouth over hers in a wet and horrifying kiss.

After a few seconds that felt to her like forever, he dropped her down just as suddenly as he'd picked her up, and immediately seemed to lose his confidence. "Don't tell anyone, okay? This is our secret." He stood awkwardly for a moment as if he didn't know what to do next, then without another word he turned and walked quickly out the driveway, picking up his empty pail on the way.

Simonne stood at the barn door, stunned. Then her heart started to pound, and she ran for the safety of the house. By the time she rushed through the back door to Randy, reading quietly at the kitchen table, she'd begun to shake and cry. "What's happened?" he asked, again and again frantically, his hands on her shoulders. "What's wrong?" She wouldn't, couldn't answer, loud wrenching sobs taking her breath away as she leaned against the counter for support. Randy ran for the church and their mother.

Sheila tore back in panic, slammed open the screen door, and wrapped her arms around Simonne. "It's okay, I'm here," she repeated over and over. "Where are you hurt? Did you fall? Did a bee sting you? Did you see a snake and get scared?" She checked for injuries as she held Simonne in her arms and rocked her like a baby, soothing and stroking until Simonne had calmed enough to tell her the story. "I should have told him how much I weigh," whispered Simonne.

"NO! You didn't do anything wrong. It's not your fault." Sheila gently set Simonne down on a chair, picked up the phone, and called the police.

The Ontario Provincial Police cruiser pulled into the driveway soon after Sheila's call, and a large officer stepped out, straightened his cap as he took in his surroundings, and came to the back door. He squatted down to Simonne's height as he calmly listened to her story, and then took some information from Sheila. He had a good idea of exactly where to go and came back not long after with a man in the back seat of his car. He gripped him firmly by the arm and brought him into the kitchen. "Is this the man who asked you for the water?"

"Yes," nodded Simonne, sheltering half behind her mother, afraid to look at anything except the floor.

Sheila took a step away from Simonne and towards the accused man. There, in her own sunny kitchen on a hot July afternoon, she stood toe to toe with the predator who had assaulted her child. A head shorter than he was, her black eyes flashing and her jaw clenched, she jabbed her finger at his chest.

"How dare you!?" she spat out. "I've seen men like you before. Do you know what they'd do to you in the army? You'd be torn apart. You disgust me! We fought a war to make the world a better place, not for animals like you to put your filthy hands on a child." Her rage was delivered in her precise English voice, no tears or shouting, while anger and indignation radiated off her rigid body. She would have torn him apart to protect her kids and he knew it, standing with his head down and his shoulders slumped.

The policeman took the man by the arm again, escorted him back to the car, and told Sheila he'd report back to her later.

In the 1950s, an assault like this was handled differently. Sheila and Brownie were advised to "let the child forget and move on," so the incident of the man with the water pail was never raised again after that day, and it slowly faded from Simonne's memory. Life carried on. And although Sheila never forgot, eventually the experience of that day was pushed to the back of her mind too. Other more pressing concerns absorbed her energy and attention.

* * * * * * * * *

For years, an awareness had been growing in Sheila that there was something missing in her life, something spiritual and fundamental that she couldn't clearly express. It gnawed at her.

Catholicism had always played an important part in the O'Carroll family. Sheila's Irish father was a staunch supporter of the Catholic church, and her mother had abandoned an Anglican upbringing for Catholicism, risking alienation from her own family. As a child, the church had been central to Sheila's family's life, and although some of her siblings had since abandoned it, Agnes, the person she admired the most, was still a practising Catholic. Sheila missed it. She'd made a quick decision when she married because she thought she was supposed to adopt her husband's religion, but as she moved closer to her fortieth birthday, she regretted leaving the church of her childhood and ached for its comfort and familiar warmth. The austere coldness of Protestantism failed to meet her spiritual needs.

Sheila finally found the courage to voice her feelings to her best friend Joyce Bridge. "I don't know what to do. Every time I drive past the church I feel like I'm missing something, I feel left out. I think about this all the time now, and I want to cry. "

"Then do something about it!" Joyce said firmly. "Find out where you have to start. Talk to Brownie. He'll understand. He must sense you're unhappy." Joyce didn't laugh at her or tell her to forget such a crazy idea and with that encouragement Sheila decided to move ahead. Her next step had to include her husband.

"Of course I get it, Sheila!" Brownie said, putting his arm around her. "I've known for a long time that something was wrong, but I didn't know what it was. So what if you don't like the United Church? It doesn't matter to me. I don't care what church you go to! I'll do whatever I have to if it makes you happy."

"Are you absolutely sure?" she asked him. "This could be a long process and I don't know what your parents will think of this."

"It doesn't matter what anyone thinks," Brownie reassured her.

The Catholic Church, mired in tradition, didn't immediately give Sheila such a warm response, and she hadn't expected one. Sheila knew the challenges she'd face. Nothing had changed for centuries. It was the same male hierarchy Sheila had known as a child. The priest was the ultimate authority. Mass was still celebrated in Latin in a shadowy ritual where women were secondary. Post-war social upheaval, the voices of the feminist movement, and the demand for civil rights had yet to reach the Catholic Church. Despite how forward-thinking Sheila was in other areas of her life, she was returning to mystical, ages-old traditions, hoping to recapture the spirituality she had been missing.

The local priest in Arthur quickly threw up his hands. "Oh my, you'll have to go to the Archdiocese in Guelph. I don't have the authority to deal with something as big as this." As Sheila had anticipated, the Archdiocese confirmed that her civil marriage in Ghent was not recognized by the Church and she had been living in sin with Brownie and their four children. It was going to be a long, tough road, made more so by the guilt and shame that came with every step of the process.

To prove she'd once really been a Catholic, Sheila contacted her old parish in Coventry for a copy of her original baptism certificate. Remarkably, the records had survived Coventry's bombs and she was able to produce it. Then came a series of confessions to repent and ask forgiveness. Months passed as the required approvals moved up the chain of command until finally there was only one box left to tick. Sheila and Brownie had to be married in the church and to promise that any unlikely future children would be Catholic. After more than fifteen years together, their union was finally going to be official and blessed.

On the evening of their "second wedding," Brownie exchanged his faded work clothes for his suit and tie. Sheila styled her hair, carefully applied her lipstick, and pinned on her cameo. Being dressed up for a special event midweek made the occasion seem all the more unusual and compounded their nervousness. As they set off down the highway to the basilica of Our Lady Immaculate in Guelph, Brownie joked to break the tension. "C'mon Sheila, let's make an honest woman of you!"

They returned a few hours later, officially married. Again. Brownie reached up into the kitchen cabinet and took down the whiskey. They rarely had a drink during the week, but this was a very special occasion and deserved a celebration. He poured them each a shot, passed Sheila her glass, and touched his rim on hers with a grin, happy to have helped make this happen. "Here's to my new wife." Sheila smiled at him as she took a sip. "And here's to us." A weight was lifted from her shoulders. She had reclaimed an important part of who she was.

But still, many months later, when the glow of the re-marriage had faded, and her weekly attendance at mass had become routine rather than special, the undefined restlessness crept back. Sheila recognized that returning to her church hadn't brought back the hoped-for security and peace of her child-hood. She was now in her forties, healthy and energetic, in the prime of her life, and her inner voice kept whispering *You can do more than this.* The diaper days were over, her kids were all in school, and the domestic routine of the 1950s had lost its appeal. She needed something more mentally stimulating.

That "something" fell into Sheila's lap the summer Randy joined the army cadets. "Hey Mom, I saw a poster today at the armouries," he told her. "Did you know they're recruiting reserve members? Part-time, one evening a week. I think I'm gonna continue, after the summer. Why don't you sign up too?"

"Me? What would I do? My last military job was driver/mechanic, and I don't think they'll be looking for a housewife to do that!" It was an entic-ing opportunity, but Sheila worried that she had no skills to offer. "Oh for heaven's sake Sheila, just go," Brownie encouraged. "I'll be here to take care of the kids, and you and Randy can drive together if you're worried about the winter roads. You know you'll love it." He had no interest himself in the mili-tary and never had, but he knew how much she missed her days in the army.

"I hope they don't put me into some kind of clerical position. I haven't touched a typewriter since before the war, and even then I could only use two fingers. I'm so rusty!"

As she had feared, a desk job was exactly what she got. She was a woman in the 1960s and that was the role women were given. The military, even its reserve ranks, was nothing if not traditional.

It was just a few hours each week, but the time back in uniform left Sheila happy and energized. "I had such a lovely chat tonight with the Major," she reported to Brownie one evening when she got home. "When he learned I was posted to Belgium at the end of the war, he kept asking questions. He was so interested in what we did there he kept me talking most of the evening."

It was not long after, in early 1963, when Brownie came home from work with news that would change everything. "My job at the Co-op is being chopped," he announced as he took off his old cap and brushed back his hair. "They're cutting the milking machine end of it, and they don't have anything else to offer me. I'll have to find another job somewhere else." He let out a big breath. "They said there are openings in other towns and they can help me, but I don't like it. I don't want to move." Brownie wasn't good at talking about his feelings, but he didn't need to say much. His body language, his slumped shoulders and downturned face, said it for him.

Sheila saw things differently. What Brownie viewed as a huge challenge she saw as an opportunity. "Don't worry," she assured him. "This will be exciting! Maybe we can find a bigger town, better schools, something I can do."

As the weeks passed and they looked at job openings and options for moving, the most intriguing in Sheila's view was the Co-op in Peterborough. It was on the other side of the province and they'd never even been there, but she urged Brownie to take a serious look at it. The manager was keen to have him join the staff, even hinting there might be a pension plan in the near future. That had been a major worry for Sheila, what they would do when Brownie could no longer work. And then, when she heard there was a new university in Peterborough, she was hooked.

"Brownie, Trent University has just opened! What an excellent opportunity for the kids."

"But Sheila, it's at least a three hour drive from Mount Forest," he protested. "We won't get up home very often, and when we do we'll have to stay for a weekend. Are you going to be willing to do that? When am I going to see Mother and Dad and the rest of my family?" Except for his years in the army, Brownie had never lived more than a few miles from the family farm and moving to the other side of the province held no appeal for him. Doing so would mean no more weekly Sunday dinners and drop-in visits to his mother, and he was reluctant to give that up.

"Of course I'll visit Mount Forest!" Sheila assured him. "We can make it an adventure and even do some exploring on the way sometimes. It just won't be as often."

Brownie didn't entirely believe her, and his concern was grounded in experience. Increasingly, Sheila had begun to resist his expectation that every holiday and every Sunday would be spent with his mother. "Go by yourself if you must go," she had said more and more often over the past few years. "I don't care. I'm staying home with the kids. We saw your mother last week."

Finally, after a few months of uncertainty, reality decided for them. Despite Brownie's reluctance to leave the home area he loved so much, no other good offers had come along. And so, in the summer of 1963, Brownie relocated to Peterborough on his own. He rented a room in a boarding house and started his new job and a real estate search, making the three hour commute back to Rothsay on the weekends. Meanwhile, Sheila packed up the old house while she made plans and dreamed of a life in a big city with new opportunities. She'd done it before and she knew she could do it again. As much as anything, the simple *idea* of change energized her.

The move meant leaving behind everything they knew. There would be no more Friday meetings with the Overseas Club or Saturday night dances at the Legion with their Rothsay friends. No old neighbours to share a chat over a cup of tea. It meant finding new schools, new doctors and dentists. Despite Sheila's optimism, it would not be simple.

The house Brownie eventually found was about five miles out of the city on a rural road at the end of a small subdivision of wartime houses. A storey and a half, painted pink and white, it was built into a hill, so the garage took up half the basement. The main door opened directly into the bright and sunny kitchen, off which was the only bathroom. There were just three bedrooms, a very small one on the main floor and two larger ones upstairs, with sloping ceilings from the angle of the roof. Closet space was almost non-existent.

What this property did offer was three acres of land, a small barn in good condition, and a fenced field, all of which were very important to Brownie. His priorities had always been clear. He would never be happy in a city house even if he had found one they could afford. Out of necessity, this place had to be purchased without Sheila's personal inspection.

On a beautiful sunny day in late August 1963, as the moving van pulled away from Rothsay, Sheila and all four kids followed behind in the family car. "Wave goodbye," Sheila told them, "Good-bye school! Good-bye Smiths' General Store! Good-bye Rothsay!" Her excitement was contagious, and the long drive passed quickly with happy chatter. The anticipation of a big new adventure grew as they came closer to their destination.

Three hours later when they pulled into the driveway behind the moving van, Sheila became quiet, her smile fading and her enthusiasm quickly evaporating. As she stepped out of the car she took in the set of cracked steps up to the kitchen door, an unkempt flowerbed, and a sad, sagging woodshed attached to the house. It was not the cute country property she had envisioned. It was dirty and neglected. She wanted to cry. "Oh Brownie," she said, "why didn't you tell me it was this bad?"

"I told you we'd have to do some work to fix it up," he fumbled. "And this was all we could afford, remember? Houses are a lot more expensive here." He had been worried about Sheila's reaction and knew she'd built up such hopes about moving to a city.

It had been a long day. The movers wanted to get unloaded and be gone, but in the midst of the chaos of boxes and furniture dumped everywhere, Sheila shouted "STOP!" Tired and angry, she was determined to do a walk-through before anything else was done. "Get rid of that filthy linoleum before we move any kids' beds into these rooms." Afraid of bed bugs and other crawly things, she wouldn't let the movers go any further until the floor was thoroughly cleaned with Dettol. "Find the mops and pails," she ordered, and pulled out the few cleaning supplies she had kept after leaving Rothsay. The house there had been left spic and span for the new owners, and she was horrified that this one was not. She scrubbed the whole upstairs before moving on to the kitchen cupboards, and then made sure the bathroom was thoroughly clean. The movers, Brownie, and the kids tiptoed carefully around her.

What had started as a joyous adventure on moving day ended in exhaustion and disappointment many miles and many hours later. Sheila sat at the re-assembled kitchen table that night, dirty and overwhelmed, with all the yet to be unpacked boxes around her. "Hey Mom," said Simonne, with the innocence of a thirteen-year-old. "Now that we've got all our furniture in here, it looks like home!" Sheila finally smiled. "You're right. It does." It was a story she repeated often in the coming years. Home was where you made it.

Sheila never really warmed up to that house, and didn't spend much effort in improving it. There was no desire, and no budget anyway. Despite that, it quickly became a comfortable family home, crowded with six people. It lacked privacy, but more often than not it was the site of laughter and love triumphing over conflict and tears. It became the place where Sheila was to face more serious challenges and upheavals in her life.

CHAPTER 15
MORE THAN A HOUSEWIFE:
1964

Wanted: Mature women to supervise female adolescents in a secure setting. Must be willing to work shifts.

It was a small advertisement, posted in the "Help Wanted" section of the *Peterborough Examiner* in early 1964, and Sheila might have missed it if she hadn't been reading the local paper cover to cover as she always did. She had never heard of The Training School for Girls in Lindsay, just a thirty-minute drive along Highway 7 through pretty farm country. It was a sort of reform school for troubled and runaway teenagers, exactly the kind of place Sheila jokingly warned her children they might end up in one day if they didn't behave.

"Look at this, Brownie," she pointed out the section she'd torn from the paper. "This is interesting. What would you think if I applied for this? It's not far up the road and the extra money would be lovely."

"What about the kids?" he replied. "Who's going to look after them if you're not here?" Brownie hadn't accepted the idea of a wife with a job and he wasn't the only one. At that time, even Dear Abby was still advising married women that they already had a job—at home.

Sheila bristled. "I've been home by myself all day for the last two years since Scott and Holly started school! You all leave every morning for school and work, and you don't come home for eight hours. Here I am alone, I don't know anyone, and I never do anything! How many times can I vacuum the same rooms? I'll soon be daft from boredom!"

"What about the summers? What about getting the kids off to school in the morning?" he retorted, knowing that she'd made up her mind already and he didn't really have much of a say.

"Randy and Simonne can put the twins on the bus before they leave for school and they can be home before the twins get back. And Simonne's still too young for a summer job, so she can watch them in the holidays if I'm not here. The twins are eight, not babies. And it's shifts so I wouldn't be gone every day." Sheila'd had quite enough of sitting at home. *But first I have to* get *the job,* she thought, not voicing her uncertainty out loud. *What have I got to offer?*

Aside from a couple of years in her late teens when she'd been a clerk at Barclay's Bank in England, and a few weeks as a fill-in janitor at the Rothsay school (which didn't end well), her stint in the army was her longest employment history. Sheila had spent almost twenty years as "just" a housewife and mother and was worried that wasn't enough to fill up a resume. *I might not be good enough for this, or any, job,* she thought as she filled out the application form. *Is being enthusiastic, healthy, and knowing how to spell going to be enough?*

It was. She made a good impression at her interview and was appointed as a probationary employee, starting on May 25th, 1964. Her excitement at stepping into the working world was only slightly dampened by her strange experience at the compulsory medical.

"It was the oddest thing," she said that evening as she was putting dinner on the table and telling Brownie and the kids about her first day at work. "I had to take off my clothes, ALL my clothes, and leave them in the change room. They didn't give me anything to cover up, not even a little hospital gown. There I sat, on a cold metal chair on my bare bottom." Holly and Scott giggled in surprise at the image of their proper mother's bare bottom for all the world to see. "I sat with my arms wrapped around my bosoms to try to stay warm, until the doctor came in. He just handed me a smock and said to put it on. No explanation or apology."

Dignified and proper in a stiff British way, Sheila found this more than odd; in fact, she thought it was shockingly unnecessary and very bizarre. "I've had physicals in the army, and I've delivered four kids, but this was quite extraordinary, even humiliating. Do you suppose they were trying to make sure I was really a woman? Or make sure I really wanted the job? Or show me who was in charge?" she added. "I started to look around to see if there was a hidden camera somewhere and if other people were watching me too." She laughed. "I sound crazy, don't I?"

"No, you don't," said Randy, embarrassed for his mother and her description of the indignity imposed on her.

"Wow, it sounds like a TV show!" chirped up Simonne, oblivious to her mother's discomfort but loving the drama. She hoped to hear more of this fascinating world of bad girls, and over the next few months Sheila didn't disappoint her. As the summer rolled by, she often came home with interesting tales.

"Today I stopped an escape!" Sheila announced just a few weeks after she'd started work. "I watched two girls tossing a teddy bear back and forth for hours, never letting it out of their possession and I just sensed something was up. This went on most of the day until one of them put it down for a moment and I had a chance to grab it. Guess what!? There was a key hidden in it, stolen from one of the keepers!"

"Good work Mom! Will this be on the news tonight?" asked Simonne. Sheila laughed. "I don't think so. I reported it my supervisor and she took over. But I'm sure the director will be pleased with my vigilance."

The next day when she returned to work, all Sheila's pleasure in a job well done quickly vanished. Her supervisor had taken full credit for preventing the escape, as if she alone had found the key. She hadn't mentioned Sheila at all in her report.

"I can't put my finger on what makes me uncomfortable at work," she told Brownie some months later. "I guess I expected things to be more professional somehow. It feels like the rules keep changing depending on who's around. Sometimes things just don't smell right, if you know what I mean." Brownie wasn't much help. He occasionally groused to Sheila about work or his manager, but had never confronted an issue or quit a job. He kept his head down and stayed out of trouble, and that was the only advice he could pass on to her. "There must be a reason for what they do," he told her. "It's not your place to question what's going on." That suggestion fell on deaf ears.

Some of the training school inmates Sheila supervised were runaways as young as twelve, from broken homes and poverty. Some were abandoned. Some girls had learning disabilities. A few were streetwise young sex workers. Most were simply trying to survive. Regardless of their life experiences or problems, they were all subject to the same reform school rules and rigid structure, including the use of isolation cells. When the behavior of a resident became too challenging, she was put into a small bare room, all her clothes removed and replaced with a hospital style smock, but no underwear. She was given nothing with which to hurt or amuse herself, not even a book. Sheila's job was to observe her through a little window, without contact or conversation. "Can't I give her something to read?" Sheila asked her boss. "She's cold. Is it okay to pass a blanket through to her?" The answers were always no.

Sheila believed there were more effective ways to engage these girls and change their behavior without locking them in isolation or making them scrub the gym floor with a toothbrush. To her, that was pointless and did more harm than good. "I picture you in that cell," she told Simonne, now fifteen and challenging authority, "and it makes me sad. I'm frightened about what might happen to you or your friends. It's too easy to end up there." Simonne laughed, confident she was far too smart to fall into that trap. "Oh Mom, you worry too much as usual."

As Sheila became more aware of the dynamics of the training school, she began to observe interactions between the young residents and male staff which she found unsettling. Favors were given to some girls but not to others. It was hard to ignore the coziness between some staff and residents, but it was equally difficult to put her finger on just what it was that spiked her senses. She stayed silent for a while, but finally decided to make an appointment with the director to tell him her concerns.

"Don't do it," Brownie said when she told him her plans. "You're sticking your nose in where it doesn't belong."

"No, you're wrong." Sheila brushed off his advice. "I have a responsibility to report issues I see, and they'll thank me for it."

"I was very respectful," she told Brownie the next evening after her meeting. "The director seemed glad that I had talked to him. He did tell me that sometimes things were not what they appeared to be, but he was still interested in what I had to say. He thanked me when I left and said he'd look into it. I know I did the right thing." Brownie said nothing. He knew bosses didn't appreciate being told what was wrong and how to fix it.

As the weeks went by and Sheila had heard nothing further from the director, she asked to see him again. There had been no evidence of changing practices and no one had mentioned anything about her concerns in staff meetings or instructions. This time the director was much cooler. "I told you I'd look into it, Mrs. Eccles, and I have. I don't know what kind of a response you expected, but I'm not required to report back to you. I think it's best if you just stick to what your job is and leave the rest to your supervisors and me."

It's obvious he's not going to change anything, Sheila told herself as she drove home that day, more annoyed than rebuked. *He's worked there a long time and he has his favorites who like things the way they've always been. I'll have to talk to someone else.*

Sheila had insisted her children's milk be pasteurized, fought to improve safety at a one-room school, and persistently confronted racism wherever she found it, but these were little battles she had a chance of winning. Her twenty years as a housewife hadn't prepared her to take on an entrenched bureaucracy, despite how well intentioned she was. Sheila was naïve.

Ignoring the director's warning to keep her ideas to herself, Sheila made an appointment to see a more senior bureaucrat in Toronto. She took a day off work to be there, her hopes high and feeling confident that she was about to contribute to important changes. She hadn't anticipated that the director would get to his bosses first to defend his management of the training school and to express his concerns about his employee Sheila. As a result, the reception she received was not what she had expected. Ushered into a room to face three senior managers, she was told she was no longer suitable for the job, but was offered the chance to resign with a reference rather than be dismissed. No one was interested in hearing the list of concerns she'd painstakingly prepared in advance.

I thought they'd want to my input, she thought afterward. *I don't get it. Why am I fired for trying to make things better? What did I do wrong?*

Questions without answers filled her head on the long drive home. Sheila returned in shock, diminished and saddened.

It was decades later, in the 1970s and 80s, when finally all Ontario training schools closed, followed by a string of legal challenges for what the courts ruled to be "cruel and sadistic abuse". The government was ordered to pay compensation to the survivors. Sheila had been right, long before it was okay to be a whistleblower.

After less than two years of working at the training school, Sheila found herself home alone again. She stared at the four walls of her kitchen and wondered what had happened. Her thoughts went over and over her dismissal. Disappointment and humiliation evolved into anger and resentment. *How can doing the right thing be the wrong thing?* she asked herself over and over. *Why would none of those powerful men in Toronto listen to me?*

No one was listening to her at home either. After the initial shock, the story was over. The kids went on with their lives in the self-absorbed way of youth. Although she tried to explain her feelings to Brownie, it was pointless. He didn't want her to be unhappy, but he didn't have the capacity to help her, and in truth he felt she had only herself to blame. He had warned her to shut up. "You have to know when to let things go, Sheila. Sometimes you're just too stubborn for your own good," he told her in exasperation.

"And if you don't stick up for what you think is right, nothing will ever change!" She bit back the rest of her tirade, knowing it wouldn't make any difference. Her only option was simply to carry on with her usual stiff upper lip as she had done with every other disappointment in her life.

Sheila was clearing the dishes off the dinner table one evening in early 1966 when she said in an off-hand way, "I'm having some tests at the hospital tomorrow. I need you to drop me off there in the morning, Brownie, and pick me up afterwards".

"Tests for what?"

"Just routine. Nothing to worry about." She turned her back and made it clear she didn't want further discussion.

The next morning as they left the house, the kids rushed out the door to get to school and on with the day, not giving much thought to what Sheila was doing. "See you later, Mom," Holly and Scott called out as they ran for the bus. "See you," she said, as she was getting in the car. *I hope.* It was taken for granted she'd be home again at suppertime, as usual. Nothing seemed out of the ordinary. Brownie drove her to the hospital and left her at the front door. "See you this afternoon, I guess," he said as Sheila got out of the car. "Yes, after work," she instructed. There was no kiss good-bye.

Sheila wasn't there when the kids got home from school, and much later, when Brownie walked in the door she wasn't with him either. His usual cheerfulness was missing and his face was tired and worried. "Where's Mom?" Holly asked, always sensitive to moods and changes. She knew something was amiss.

"Your mother's in the hospital," Brownie said, "and Randy, as soon as we've had a bite to eat, I want you come back with me to see Mom. She has to stay overnight."

"Why? What's the matter? Is she sick?" The kids pressed Brownie for more details.

He shook his head. "I don't know. I hope we'll find out more tonight."

Earlier, when Brownie went to the hospital after work as instructed, expecting to pick up Sheila at the door where he'd left her, he was directed to the Admitting Department. "I'm here to pick up my wife?" he said tentatively to the clerk, confused that Sheila was not where she was supposed to be. "Mrs. Eccles is on the surgical floor, sir," he was told. "They'll give you more information there." In his dusty green work shirt and pants and his heavy boots, he felt out of place walking through the clean hospital. Sheila hadn't warned him about any of this. He finally found the right floor and stood before the nurses' desk, twisting his cap in his hand. "I'm looking for my wife, Sheila Eccles."

"She's going to be in room 406. Down the hall." The nurse didn't glance away from her paperwork. Brownie stood there, clearly confused. "What's happened?" he asked. "I was supposed to pick her up after a test." The nurse finally looked up. "She's had a major operation, Mr. Eccles. For breast cancer. She's just coming out of the anesthetic." She thought it strange that the husband didn't seem to know anything about this. "Come back later this evening," she said, more gently. "You can see her when she's more awake from the surgery".

Sheila had found a lump in her breast a week or two earlier, but told no one except the family doctor. Her sister Eileen had been through breast cancer, so Sheila had an idea of what to expect. She knew if the biopsy came back positive she would immediately undergo the removal of her breast and any other tissue which might be affected. She had had to authorize the potential major surgery prior to being anesthetized. Right up to the point when Brownie dropped her off at the hospital, she had told him nothing about this. She hadn't shared her worry or her fears, even with her husband.

The surgeon had performed a radical mastectomy, which at that time was the routine approach to eliminating cancer cells. Sheila's entire breast, much of the underlying chest wall muscle, and the lymph nodes on one side had been removed. It was a necessary surgery, but a devastating mutilation just the same. She was forty-seven years old.

When the whole family was finally able to visit a few nights later, Sheila was sitting up in her hospital bed. Her upper body was wrapped firmly in bulky bandages, over her chest and across one shoulder, but she chatted away like it was a social visit. "I'm sorry if I scared you," she said, smiling at each child. "Maybe I should have told you beforehand, but I didn't want anyone to worry." Holly said nothing, leaning against Brownie for support, trying not to cry. "Does it hurt?" Scott asked, staring at the huge lump of medical wrappings around half his mother's body. "It's not too bad," Sheila said, trying not to wince when she moved. She acted as if everything was fine, or would be, as if nothing had changed. She was convincing, and her kids saw only what they wanted to, the spunky and unsinkable mother they had always known.

Just before she was scheduled for discharge, Sheila found out she needed to go to St. Margaret's hospital in downtown Toronto for radiation treatment to kill any remaining cancer cells. It was an aggressive treatment which meant more weeks away from home.

Sheila remained staunchly upbeat; she never complained of pain, never spoke about the disfigurement of her body. To her children, and to Brownie, she put on a brave face. The trip to Toronto and the upcoming stay in the patient lodge were portrayed as a big adventure, a bit of a vacation from the routine at home. "This is like the joke we used to tell in England," she told Holly with a laugh. "A mother's only holiday is going to the hospital to have a baby."

It wasn't the holiday Sheila pretended it would be, and when she finally returned after a few weeks at St. Margaret's, her body was starkly marked with the radiation map of harsh lines and dots. Following the physical shock of the surgery, and the long frightening rounds of radiation, Sheila faced the daunting challenge of regaining her strength mentally as well as physically, and trying to put her life back together.

Months later, after surgery and radiation, Sheila could no longer raise her arm without severe pain. Doing anything from washing clothes to making beds was agony, but there seemed to be little treatment beyond pain killers. "I told the doctor I'm not spending my life doped up," she said angrily to Brownie, "I'd rather be in pain. And how am I supposed to drive if I take those? I'm not going to let myself become a drug addict." Brownie had no answer. Finally, Sheila reluctantly agreed to another surgery so that her arm could be manipulated and moved, muscles and tendons forcibly "unfrozen". Still in serious pain afterwards, she devised her own physiotherapy program. She would move her arm slowly up the wall, a little more each day, marking her progress with a pencil line until she could reach above her head.

"Brownie, could you find a rod to put across this door frame so I can stretch out my arm?" He was happy to finally be able to help, and installed a chin up bar. When Sheila was strong enough, she began to cautiously pull herself up on it a few times each day, slowly increasing the pressure until she could support her weight with just the tips of her toes touching the floor. "Hey kids, look at me! I'm going to run away to the circus and be an acrobat!"

"I can do ten chin-ups," Scott challenged her. "What about you?"

The kids cheered her on, glad to see their mother's good spirits returning. After months of pain, self-discipline, and perseverance, Sheila was finally able to move normally.

There were other challenges, ones she couldn't describe, ones not so easily fixed. Her medical knowledge came from her well-worn and dated encyclopedia, the newspaper articles she consumed so voraciously, and her nurse sisters when she chose to share her problems with them. However, none of these resources addressed the emotional changes that swept through her after her cancer. She began to worry about how long she had left and, even more, about her quality of life in the coming years.

Is this all there is to my life? Sheila worried. *This isn't what I dreamed for my future. There has to be more, or what's the point to all of this?*

CHAPTER 16
WHAT NEXT?
1960's

"ARE YOU EVEN LISTENING TO ME?"

Sheila screamed at Brownie in frustration, banging a wooden spoon on the countertop. He was sitting in his usual place at the kitchen table, tired and dusty after his day at the Co-op, sweat stains dried on his faded work shirt, his shoulders slumped and his head down. Dinner was over, but Sheila's tirade about bills and other household problems had started before the meal, continued through it, and was now escalating in the face of Brownie's silence. There was nothing more he could say to make it right. Then, as Sheila's rage reached its pinnacle, she flung the spoon across the kitchen at him. Brownie jumped up from his chair much faster than his fatigue suggested was possible, grabbed Sheila roughly around the waist and arms without a word and hauled her the few strides into their bedroom. He dumped her on the bed, and immediately turned back into the kitchen, shaking with unspoken fury.

Randy, Simonne, and Holly had quickly dispersed after dinner, wanting to be out of range of their mother's anger, but nine-year-old Scott was still at the table, waiting for his dad to finish so they could go and feed the chickens together. As he witnessed the scene between his parents he burst into frightened tears.

A couple of minutes later Sheila came out of the bedroom as if nothing had happened. "Oh, you've put out my cigarette," she said calmly to Brownie, as though she'd just been called away for something routine. She turned then to little Scott, still sobbing, and said gently, "I won't do that anymore in front of you kids." It was a sort of apology. The incident was over and never spoken of again.

As if cancer and the resulting disfiguring surgery hadn't done enough damage physically and emotionally to Sheila, menopause provided the knockout punch. It arrived with a vengeance, pouring gasoline on all the fires smouldering within her. In addition to hot flashes and sudden hemorrhages, all discreetly hidden, her existing feelings of alienation and anger grew rapidly following her return from St. Margaret's. In the space of a couple of years, she'd evolved from a healthy and happy woman in her prime to someone who'd lost her job, parts of her body, and her sense of who she was. Sheila was floundering.

A drama began to unfold in the pink and white house with Brownie and the kids as the audience. Sometimes they were observers on the sidelines, but often they participated in the scenes, whether they wanted to or not. Sheila's unhappiness was obvious to them all, but they didn't understand it and could do nothing to help. Sheila didn't, and couldn't name her feelings, but the clear signal that something was very wrong was expressed in two ways. Sometimes it was the fight mechanism. Sometimes it was flight.

"If you were ever here," Sheila railed at Brownie as she stood over him jabbing her finger at him, "or ever took control over what these kids do . . . ." It was the end of a hot summer day, and through most of it Sheila had been at the receiving end of a child's relentless whining for permission to do something that was not allowed. Sheila, fed up with the constant grind of the conflict, spilled her frustration onto Brownie, blaming him for everything that was wrong. He too was tired, not just from the heat and his long day at work, but from trying and failing to figure out how to do anything right for Sheila.

In the middle of her long tirade, he rose halfway from his chair, shot out his arm, and slapped her across the face. Sheila gasped as she stumbled back a couple of steps until she hit the kitchen counter and found her balance, then took a few deep breaths, straightened to her full height, and silently walked out of the room. One arm of her blouse had ripped open. In the sudden silence of the room Brownie stood absolutely still, ashen faced, looking as if he was the one who'd been struck. He turned and went out the door to the barn without saying a word.

It was Brownie's quiet calmness that had attracted Sheila in the first place, just as her extroverted energy had appealed to him. Two decades on, those same qualities were pushing them apart, Brownie silent and non-confrontational, Sheila angry and aggressive.

In desperation, Brownie finally reached out to their family doctor. "I'm worried sick," he told Dr. Speller. "Sometimes I'm so angry at Sheila when she's screaming at me, I don't know what I might end up doing to her."

"Then get out of the house until you can calm down". That was the only prescription from the doctor. So, more and more Brownie retreated to the barn and the comforting silence of his animals. More and more Sheila paced the house alone with her thoughts.

"Will you PLEASE stop pretending you know everything!" Sheila screamed at Simonne in exasperation one morning in the rush of the exit for school. As usual, they were in the middle of a raging dispute about something inconsequential, a rebelling teenage daughter versus an unhappy and ill mother. The room was filled with hormones and raised voices. As Simonne turned to open the door to run for the bus, still arguing and calling out, "You're wrong," Sheila grabbed her half-full coffee cup and threw it. It smashed into the doorframe just inches from Simonne and broke into shards, the coffee dripping down the wall onto the floor. Finally silenced, Simonne slammed the door, stomped down the steps to the road, and burst into tears.

Sheila was waiting at the door when Simonne returned from school later that day, all evidence of the broken mug and coffee spill long since cleaned up. She smiled a bit sheepishly and shrugged her shoulders. "I'm so sorry. Forgive me, " Sheila said, as if to mean, *It was all my fault.* "Let's not do that again." Simonne nodded. "Okay."

Since the assault of her surgery, radiation, and menopause, sleep became elusive most nights. Sheila lay restlessly for hours in the stuffy little bedroom, looking at the ceiling and listening to Brownie snore beside her in their small double bed. Her head was filled with unvoiced thoughts and worries. *Is the cancer gone? Will the rest of my life be better? Or worse? What's going to happen to my children?* More and more often, she slipped out of bed to sit alone in the dark at the kitchen table, or to stand looking out the front window at the lights of the cars and trucks on the highway at the end of the concession road, wondering where they were going and what lives they were living, the anonymous people in those vehicles.

It didn't take long before she began to join them.

Sheila got dressed quietly in the dark, hoping not to wake anyone and have to face questions she couldn't answer. She took her purse and car keys, and left the house, softly closing the door behind her and gently shushing the dog so he wouldn't bark. It didn't matter, anyway, because Brownie was usually laying awake too, pretending to be asleep until he heard the door close and then getting up to watch her taillights disappear down the road and to worry if she would come home at all. Sometimes he felt brave enough to confront her. Standing in the bedroom door, in his bare feet and ragged pajamas, without his false teeth, he called out to her in a whisper just loud enough not to wake the kids upstairs. "What are you doing Sheila? Where are you going?" "Out," she replied curtly, not meeting his eyes. "I'm going nowhere".

Sometimes her trips were brief, sometimes she was gone for hours, coming home at dawn and finally falling asleep on the couch. Brownie was terrified of what she might do in her desperation and unhappiness, awful things he didn't want to think about as he lay awake listening for her return.

The nocturnal forays were a coping mechanism Sheila employed on and off for the rest of her life. Her comfort zone was behind the wheel, alone but not lonely, and not afraid of the darkness. After all the years of army driving, it was the place she felt most competent. She was more frightened of what was inside her than what she might meet on a nighttime road.

Brownie needn't have worried that she might kill herself. Sheila wanted to improve her life, not end it. She was too much of a fighter to give in, and deep down she held onto the hope that things would improve.

* * * * * * * * *

The only phone in the pink and white house was in the kitchen, so on the Sunday afternoon that Simonne received an unusual call from the mother of her best friend Debbie, it was impossible for Sheila and Brownie not to overhear her side of the conversation. They tried not to eavesdrop, but as the call proceeded, it became clear to both of them that whatever was being said was upsetting Simonne. They exchanged a confused glance at first, and then more concerned looks as their eyes met.

When fifteen-year-old Simonne had decided she was a hippy, Sheila and Brownie went along with it. The bohemian clothes, lank hair, and terrible folk singing might have been an embarrassment for most parents, but not Sheila and Brownie. A raised eyebrow, a shrug, and a knowing smile between them had been the extent of their reaction. No criticism was voiced. Their attitude signalled for Simonne to "try her wings".

Debbie's mother was not so tolerant. "You're an embarrassment," she said to Simonne on the phone. "You should see yourself. You look ridiculous and I don't know why your mother doesn't put a stop to this." When Simonne said nothing, she continued, "I don't want Debbie to be friends with you until you start to act like the other girls. You're not welcome in my home until then."

When Simonne finally hung up the phone she burst into tears.

"You know you don't have to do what Debbie's mother tells you," Brownie said gently when Simonne told them what had been said. "We don't care what she thinks. Why would you?"

"Make your own decisions. Be who you are. You're not doing anything wrong." Sheila added. Their message was empowering. It turned a devastating teenage moment into a lesson in self-confidence. They had difficulty discussing their own emotions, but when it came to values, dialogue was not required. Sheila and Brownie were on the same page.

Like feelings, sex was another topic that was not for everyday discussion around the family dinner table. Properly English, Sheila didn't bring up the subject. It was something that happened behind closed doors, and she didn't feel the need to openly or casually talk about it. Bawdy jokes at the Eccles farm were generally met with an appropriately Queen Elizabeth look that said, "*We are not amused.*" Sheila's comments about sex were rare and cryptic.

"Ohhh, he can put his shoes under my bed anytime!" Sheila joked when the conversation came around to a particularly handsome man on TV. Brownie laughed out loud. Simonne and Randy's mouths dropped open in shock.

"I hope there won't be any hand-holding nonsense going on," she said to teenage Simonne as she was leaving the house on a date with her boyfriend. It was the closest she came to a mother-daughter "don't get pregnant" conversation, and was met with considerable eye-rolling. Brownie just shook his head as usual and ruefully looked away.

If sex was not a topic for discussion, sexuality was definitely off the table when the kids were around. Sheila and Brownie never talked about men who liked men, or women who preferred women. Homosexuality was illegal and hidden until Justice Minister Pierre Elliot Trudeau introduced a bill in late 1967 to legalize sexual acts between consenting adults, and famously commented that the state had no place in the bedrooms of the nation. Brownie and Sheila were certainly aware homosexuality existed and had known gay people in the military and elsewhere. The extent of their reaction when discussing someone "different" was a raised eyebrow and perhaps a reference to being artistic or gentle or a confirmed bachelor, never anything overtly critical. Their tolerance became quite evident in the spring of 1967.

Early that year, the elected board of the local high school announced they were firing the vice principal. He was shaking up the rural school with his flamboyant style and modern approach to engaging students, but after only a year, the school board intended to end his contract. He was immensely popular with all the students, and Simonne and her friends on the student council were outraged.

The real but unspoken rationale for his dismissal was that the VP was very obviously gay. The school board was concerned about his potential influence on vulnerable students, most of whom, like Simonne, were naïvely innocent. Sheila and Brownie had quickly summed up the situation and come to their own conclusion. Without a word spoken, they looked at each other and nodded their heads in agreement that the school board was wrong. They said nothing about his sexuality, not wanting to shatter Simonne's respect and faith in the educator who was such a positive influence. They had never met him, but had heard rumblings from some of the other parents. They ignored all that. For them, it was not a question of his sexuality, but of firing someone because of closed minds.

"Why don't you speak up about this directly to the School Board?" Sheila encouraged Simonne. "Write to them, or better yet, ask to be heard at one of their meetings. Or send a letter to the editor to voice your opinion." That had been her way of airing her discontent on many occasions in the past.

When all of Sheila's ideas failed and the school board still stubbornly refused to budge, Simonne and her friends decided to organize a picket of the school. They had seen many examples of student protests happening all over the world in the 60s, against poverty and in support of civil rights and free speech. Sheila thought the demonstration was a grand idea too, a little bit of grass roots politics. "You have to fight for what you believe in," she said. "It's important in life to speak up when you think something needs to be changed. Get out there and be counted." Brownie nodded his agreement. It was not something he would ever do, but he didn't oppose the idea.

For a couple of hours one spring morning, it became a huge event. Hundreds of high school students refused to go to classes and instead picketed to support the vice principal whose dismissal they felt was unfair. A student demonstration at a rural high school was so unusual that it was reported on the national news that night. While many parents were unhappy with their kids if they participated, Sheila and Brownie were proud of their daughter for organizing it. In the end the vice principal quietly stepped down, but the lesson of taking action remained.

In the coming years Sheila found many more occasions to encourage her children to push the limits and to be brave enough to take risks and speak up. For her, 1967 was going to be the year to do the same, starting down a road that challenged her mind and expanded her experiences.

CHAPTER 17
NOTHING STAYS THE SAME: 1967

"What do you think of this?" Sheila asked Brownie, thinking out loud. "What if I took the social services worker course at the new college? Maybe then I'd be qualified for some sort of decent job. I might even be good at it." Brownie made a non-committal and safe noise, enough to indicate he was listening.

"What have I got to lose?" she added, not expecting an answer. "I really don't need to be here all day." She was forty-eight years old, just recovered from cancer, unhappy, and at loose ends. She envisioned hope and a bit of adventure behind the doors of the new college.

By 1967, Ontario had announced the opening of a number of community colleges, including Sir Sandford Fleming. One of the attractions of moving to Peterborough in the first place had been the promise of improved opportunities for her children's education, and Sheila recognized that it was now time to take advantage of the location for herself. Ontario had also just begun to offer student loans, as well as grants to needy students, so there was no serious financial impediment to returning to school, which removed the last obvious excuse. All Sheila needed now was enough self-confidence.

That same summer, Randy left home for a banking job in Toronto. Sheila's quiet first-born was in a white collar job, just as she had been when she finished school, and while she was sad to see him leave the nest, she was also very proud of him.

"Randy, I've ironed those shirts for you so they're all ready to pack now. And I sewed on a couple of buttons that looked set to fall off."

"Thanks Mom. You didn't need to do that," he replied. Randy understood this was a big moment for Sheila. Her excitement for him and slight sadness at seeing him go was being channeled into fussing with his wardrobe.

As the oldest child, Randy was the role model for the younger three. Once, following yet another loud mother/daughter battle, he offered some valuable advice to Simonne. "How come you don't have fights with Mom?" she had asked him in frustration. "Don't argue," he replied. "Just keep quiet and then find a way to do what you want to anyway." It was how both Randy and Brownie managed to stay out of most conflicts. That strategy stood in sharp contrast to the confrontational styles of Sheila and Simonne.

There was now going to be an empty chair at the kitchen table and one less voice in the family conversations. Randy would be missed.

With the distraction of her son's departure, Sheila had left her college application to the last minute. Just before the cut-off date, she scrambled to gather together her secondary school graduation records from thirty years, a continent, and a wartime ago. The documents at Stoke Park Secondary School (for refined young ladies) had survived the war, and Sheila was able to get the proof that she had the appropriate pre-requisites.

It turned out that Sheila was in an all-woman class, social services being viewed more as a woman's career than a man's. Most of Sheila's classmates had just graduated from high school, and were young enough to be her daughters. She was one of three mature students, women like her who already had life experiences to bring to the classroom. She didn't know it then, but they would become part of her circle of lifelong contacts, playing the important role of women supporting other women.

For the past twenty-five years, Sheila had been more or less able to plan her own day and be her own boss. Aside from some brief training before she worked at the Lindsay Girls' School, her last formal educational experience had been technical and hands-on, learning how to maintain and make emergency repairs to vehicles in the war. She had not sat in a classroom in decades and had not had to work around a prescribed schedule or fit her life around the hands of the clock. "I'd forgotten how disciplined you have to be!" she commented at dinner a few weeks after classes had started. "You kids have been doing this every day and I didn't realize how much focus it takes. It's hard work!"

"Yes!" Holly, Scott, and Simonne replied together, pleasantly surprised at their mother's acknowledgement. Sheila's previous school experience had been in a structured traditional British setting, but a college classroom in the late 1960s was starkly different. "People just speak up whenever they want to!" she marveled. "In my day you had to raise your hand and wait to be asked to comment. And then you had to stand up to address the teacher." She laughed. "I'm really getting an education in more ways than one."

She knew this was going to be challenging, even daunting, but she had her enthusiasm and a bright mind. Her strength had always been on the intellectual side, reading newspapers, writing letters to the editor, debating ideas. She believed if she could harness the same self-discipline and focus she had used in the physiotherapy of her arm and still the restlessness of the last few years, she had a good chance of not just getting through, but enjoying the four semesters of her program.

Domesticity quickly took a back seat to education. Over the years, Sheila had learned enough to get by in the kitchen, and her house was always clean and tidy, but being a housewife was not her first love and she now gladly stepped away from that in favor of her studies. With her attention wrapped up in a class or her nose in a book in the library, Sheila often didn't appear at home until supper was on the table or later. The family's schedule became less and less of a priority for her. As a result, meal prep began to fall more and more to Simonne and Holly. "Oh how lovely," Sheila often said as she came through the door, "you've got dinner ready. You're all so wonderful! I didn't realize how late it was." Sheila wasn't intentionally neglecting her family; she was just confident that they could carry on without her. By default, more and more domestic tasks were taken over by Brownie and the kids. Simonne was seventeen and Scott and Holly were eleven and didn't need constant supervision. They did what they had to do. Every night after supper, with the dishes done and Sheila's plate finally cleared from the table, Brownie and the kids prepared the next day's lunches for everyone.

In assembly line style, the lunch bags were laid out in a row, an apple dropped into each one, followed by some kind of a cookie, and the sandwiches added on top. A dozen slices of bread were spread on the counter and something found in the fridge for a filling. "Don't put any butter on mine please," Holly instructed every night. "And no mayonnaise for me," Sheila added, from behind her newspaper. It became a nightly bonding experience, a few shared moments, a few laughs, and a chance to air a few gripes. Grocery shopping often fell to Brownie on Saturdays or after work, and housecleaning became a shared weekend job. No one complained. Gender-specific roles blurred as domestic tasks were shared out of necessity. Brownie was quite happy with the new arrangement, as peace, laughter, and stability fell over the household, a sharp contrast to the times of uncertainty and unhappiness in the past couple of years.

Every morning Sheila grabbed her lunch bag from the fridge, collected her books and assignments, cheerily said goodbye, and drove off to school. "See you at supper time!" she called over her shoulder as she rushed out the door. She had made a little study space for herself in a corner of the living room, and was often there late into the night after everyone else had gone to bed, tapping out an essay with two fingers on her old manual typewriter. She struggled with some subjects and excelled at others. She worried about her marks and marveled at how easily the concepts came to some of her younger classmates. For the first time since living with her family in Coventry, she had people around her all day who were just as interested as she was in debating everything from social policy and politics to fairness and religion, to the welfare state and Indigenous issues. She was happy.

Sheila had never used the term feminism, although the ideas and feelings with which she had struggled fit the concept. She just hadn't labelled it. In the early 1960s, Betty Friedan published The Feminine Mystique, challenging the post-war belief that women were fulfilled in only one way—by being a housewife and mother. Sheila hadn't read Friedan, but she was definitely resentful about the unfairness and imbalance of many aspects of a woman's life in the 50s and 60s, and the fact that men were regarded as superior. She had chafed at having no financial independence as a married woman and she was disappointed by the limited roles available to women in the post-war years of her adulthood. But up to this time, she hadn't explicitly talked about her frustrations as part of a bigger social movement, not realizing that many other women, rich and poor, felt the same. Now in college, Sheila heard many of the things she had been thinking loudly expressed by a younger generation. Finally, she felt less and less of an oddity. Nonetheless there were times when her younger classmates shocked her with their extreme points of view on issues like abortion, free love, and burning bras. Sometimes Sheila even surprised herself by arguing a more conservative viewpoint than she thought she had. "I wouldn't like my daughters to have sex with every Tom, Dick, and Harry!" she responded when the lunchroom debates turned to sexual freedom. The years of Catholic teaching in her youth were hard to forget.

Finally in her element for the first time in years, Sheila's confidence and self-esteem returned, and she began feeling physically and mentally healthy. Each time that an all-clear came back from her yearly cancer checkup, she breathed a sigh of relief. *If I can just get to the five-year point,* she told herself, *I know I'll be fine.*

When the envelope from Fleming College arrived in the mailbox in the summer of 1968 at the end of her first year, Sheila tore it open, holding her breath. "I passed!" she joyfully announced to her kids in the kitchen. "It was harder than I thought it would be," she admitted with a smile. "I wish my marks were better, but it's been a long time since I had to study for an exam. Now I know how you all feel."

"Good work Mom," they congratulated her. It was becoming fun to have a mother at school.

That summer, Scott and Holly pitched a tent on the lawn behind the house and had been sleeping out in it most nights, enjoying the freedom of camping, until one evening when a noisy thunderstorm struck. They grabbed their sleeping bags and flashlights and rushed into the house. The next morning, when they went out to check for water damage, the tent was gone. "Mom, Dad, where's our tent?" they asked as they came running back into the house. "How does a tent disappear in middle of the night in the rain?"

"I guess it must have been stolen," Brownie said. "But why didn't the dog bark if a stranger was here?" There was no immediate answer to the puzzle, but Sheila was not going to just shrug like Brownie and let it go. "I'm going to get to the bottom of this," she told them. "Someone will know something, and I know where to start asking questions."

About a mile up the road was Woody's motorcycle repair shop, well-known locally as a hang out for the local Satan's Choice motorcycle club. The neighbourhood had become used to hearing the Harleys coming and going, and to Sheila it seemed like an obvious place to start a search. "Now Sheila, I don't think that's a good idea," Brownie warned her. "You don't know these guys."

"You're a man. If you go and ask them, they won't tell you anything and they might threaten you," Sheila reasoned. "If I go, they'll think I'm just a harmless woman and they might help me."

"Those bikers will never snitch on one of their own, even if they did take the tent." Brownie replied. "And I don't think they were out on their bikes in the middle of a rainstorm. It doesn't make sense."

As usual Sheila was undeterred and determined that the next step was to consult with Woody and his clientele. Emboldened by her recent success at college, this was a challenge and an adventure she didn't want to miss. And so, on that sunny Sunday morning, she drove up and parked in front of Woody's shop, got out of the car, and walked in, chin up and shoulders back as always, past the bikers lounging there watching her arrival. "Good morning," she said cheerfully to the assembled group in her best English accent. "What lovely motorcycles! I haven't ridden one in years, but I used to ride a Royal Enfield in the war. These are much bigger. I don't know if I'd be confident or strong enough to handle one now."

A look of surprise and a hint of respect came over their faces as this middle-aged woman smiled at them. She had dared to walk into their shop and she was obviously not afraid. And she knew something about bikes.

"I'm sorry to bother you, but I'm here about my children's tent. Which one of you is Woody? I'm hoping you can help me."

"Woody just laughed," Sheila reported when she got home, unharmed. "He was ever so nice, but he said he didn't know anything about anyone stealing our tent."

"What did you expect?" Brownie said, shaking his head. "He wasn't going to tell you anything, even if he knows something."

"He promised to keep his eyes open and let me know if he heard anything. And the other young men were very pleasant. I didn't feel threatened. If you're nice to people, they're usually nice back," she added.

The tent was never recovered.

That same summer, the phone rang very late one night, waking everyone in the house. Brownie jumped out of bed knowing that a call in the middle of the night could only be bad news. He stood at the bottom of the stairs with the receiver to his ear, answering in strained monosyllables, as the kids lay awake in their beds upstairs, listening and waiting. He put the phone down gently after a couple of minutes, walked into the downstairs bedroom and lay down beside Sheila. "That was George," he whispered, "Mother's gone." After a second, he said, "Oh, Sheila," as his voice broke. "Oh, Sheila. Oh, Sheila." She put her arms around him and silently held him as he wept.

When morning finally came after a sleepless night, Brownie was a wreck, a shadow of his normally cheerful self, grey and subdued. He felt overwhelmed by the need to make plans for the family to get to Mount Forest and the funeral, something he dreaded. "What time will you be ready to leave?" he asked Sheila. "I'd like to get there as soon as we can to help out. They're waiting for me."

"I'm not going," she replied, as years of pent up resentment spilled out, her voice rising. "Why should I go to *your* mother's funeral? I couldn't go to England to the funerals of my own parents," she angrily threw at him.

He stood silently in shock for a moment, as if he'd been slapped, trying to process the idea that his wife wasn't coming with him. "I told you to go," he said softly. "I *wanted* you to go to your parents' funerals. I would have found the money somewhere but you refused. You know that." Sheila didn't reply. She turned her back and walked away, and Brownie, grief stricken and distressed, put up no further resistance.

"I don't want you driving in the emotional state you're in," Sheila told him a bit later as he was getting his only suit out of the closet and gathering together a white shirt and somber tie. He turned and looked at her. "Then how am I supposed to get there?" he asked numbly.

"Take the bus to Toronto and Randy can meet you." Sheila had clearly thought this through and had left no option for Simonne, Scott, or Holly to attend their grandmother's funeral either. Brownie said nothing, knowing the decision was made and it would be pointless to argue. A few hours later Simonne, not Sheila, drove him to the station, where he boarded the bus like an indigent traveller. Randy picked him up in Toronto, and together they drove on to Mount Forest.

"Was your father okay?" Sheila asked Simonne when she came back from the bus station. "I just couldn't do it," she added, as if she felt an explanation or apology was needed, or a justification to herself. "There'll be too much weeping and melodrama, and I can't stand it."

Sheila could express anger, raising her voice and throwing things, and it was obvious when she was happy, singing and smiling and full of energy. She wasn't afraid of child molesters or bikers or driving alone at night, but she didn't know how to express sadness or grief. Her fallback reaction to that was a stiff upper lip. No tears. Life had to go on. Avoiding demonstrations of difficult emotions had become a lifelong pattern. She had used the excuse of no money to avoid her father's funeral, and then her mother's. Just as she didn't warn her family before her cancer surgery, she didn't tell them until much later when each of her siblings had passed away, one by one, over the years. She didn't even tell the kids when Toby, the beloved old family dog, had died.

I didn't want to upset you was her standard explanation, as if somehow she was protecting them from hurt and it would be less sad to find out later. She kept the toughest emotions carefully sealed inside her.

Sheila's refusal to attend her mother-in-law's funeral was a large wound in her relationship with the Eccles. Decades after Sheila had died, Brownie's sister Evelyn asked Simonne why. "Mother was so good to her when she arrived from England," Ev said, "I think she should have been there to show her respect. And Dad always thought the world of Sheila. He was so hurt when she didn't bother to come." Simonne didn't have an answer. The Eccles family had tried their best to make Sheila feel welcome and loved, and never understood why she had purposely caused them such pain.

It took a long time for Sheila's insult to her in-laws to heal over, but eventually it did for the most part. Brownie's humiliation at his mother's funeral was forgiven eventually, but not completely forgotten. Although she never spoke of it, Sheila too finally came to see that she had made a mistake. Many years later, the arrangements she made for her own funeral sent the message that she finally understood the importance of sharing sadness and mourning.

CHAPTER 18
MORE CHANGES:
1968 TO 1971

"Better get to bed early," Sheila told Holly and Scott. "We've got to get back into good habits for when school starts next week." They moaned in protest.

It was the same every year. Sheila always insisted that the last week of summer holidays was when everyone started going to bed earlier so they could start getting up earlier in the mornings. Routine was important. She was eager to get back to school again, having missed the stimulation of her classes and the excitement of being a student. With one year left on her program, she looked forward to graduating and hopefully moving on to the working world, just like the twenty-somethings in her class.

A year had passed since Randy had moved away, and now, in late August 1968 Simonne too was leaving for university. Chafing to be independent, she had resisted any advice from Sheila about course selection, a place to live, or how to manage her student loan. After all her attempts at intervention were rejected, Sheila gave up and let Simonne make the important decisions on her own, calmly waiting to see what would happen. *Well,* she mused, *I suppose my parents must have felt something like this when I took off on my bicycle for Bournemouth. I was the same age as Simonne and I thought I was so grown up.*

Sheila hoped at the very least her letters would be welcomed so she began sending them within days of Simonne's departure. Sometimes it was a quick note scrawled late at night on a scrap of paper, talking about a little incident that had happened that day. Often it was a longer chatty letter filled with everything from details of her day at school or Scott and Holly's activities, or comments on family news or an article she'd torn from the newspaper. When she had filled the pages, she wrote along the sides of the paper in the margins, a habit from the days of using every square inch of the flimsy blue airmail stationery she sent to England. Her notes were upbeat and cheery, and often included a two dollar bill, occasionally a five, which meant she'd given up her coffee money for a few days. "I hope this helps to get you a treat." Sheila knew very well what it felt like to leave home.

When Simonne or Randy came home for a weekend visit, they were sent back with a care package, items Sheila had taken from her cupboard at the last minute and packed into a cardboard box: eggs from Brownie's chickens and potatoes from his garden, Sheila's favorite TUC English crackers, tea bags, a can of cream of celery soup. It was basic comfort food, a throw back to twenty years earlier when she had sent parcels to her parents in Coventry to augment their limited rations after the war.

The spring of 1969 brought Sheila's well-deserved graduation plus a job offer with the city's welfare department. It was exactly what she had hoped for, a position where she could work face to face with clients and where she might be able to make a difference in their lives. Assessing applications for financial assistance, she spent a lot of her working day visiting recipients in their homes to verify the information they had submitted and to provide some advice on budgets and money management. Her network grew as she coordinated with landlords, police, and other social agencies involved with the same clients.

Sheila was fifty years old, but she had the energy and motivation of a much younger woman, and she loved her job. "It's so nice to finally have my own paycheque again," she announced to the family, waving it in her hand as she came through the door at the end of the first month. "But it feels even better to know I'm doing something important. All those late nights of studying seem worth it now." Brownie nodded his agreement, pleased that the second income was going to take some of the weight off his shoulders. "I know there are limits to what I can do," she added, "but I think I can help at least some of my welfare cases to do better." She understood the worry of not having enough money to pay the bills, and she felt she could pass along the hard lessons she had learned.

Sheila had always been disgusted by bed bugs and lice, and was deathly afraid of vermin, so stepping into some of her clients' squalid homes was a challenge. Often she came home from work and immediately put her clothes in the laundry. "I'm sure they have fleas in that house," she explained with a shudder. "I always try to choose the wooden chairs if I'm asked to sit down. I'm not risking anything crawling out of the upholstery!" "Ewwhhh!" Holly said, sharing her mother's disgust. "What do you do if someone offers you a cup of tea?"

"I don't want them to think I'm turning up my nose, so if I can't find an excuse, I say yes, but then I don't drink it. How do I know if the cup is clean?" She managed this with enough finesse that her clients either didn't notice or didn't mind. What they saw was the rather proper English lady who took her time to talk to them and listen to their problems.

In fact, Sheila took lots of time. She went to work early and stayed long past when other staff had gone home. She wrote copious notes and detailed explanations, and passed along information she thought might help her clients. Her caseload included single mothers, people with addictions, recent releases from prison, and multi-generational welfare families. Some of her clients lived in the cheap rented rooms in the Grand Hotel, above the bar where the strippers performed, and Sheila had come to know the manager Mr. Green. "Good morning," she called out cheerily when she found him in his office. "Just thought I'd pop in to see how things were going. Did you get your rent on time this week?"

"Yes, thank you for making that happen," he replied as he stood up and shook her hand. It was a rough place, but she was not intimidated any more than she had been talking to the bikers at Woody's. She walked in with her shoulders back and a smile on her face, ignoring the smell of spilled beer and years of cigarette smoke, as she made her way up the dingy staircase to a shabby room.

Sheila's reputation for fairness even spread to the local watering holes. The Pig's Ear was one of Peterborough's rough blue-collar bars that had been discovered by Trent University students as a place to drink cheap beer, causing friction with the regulars who resented the influx. Tension was growing one evening between a table of university kids and a bunch of the local tough guys when one of them recognized Simonne with the students. "Hey, don't I know you? " he called over the din. "We rode on the same school bus. Is your name Eccles?"

"Yes . . ." Simonne replied cautiously.

"Your mother's the welfare lady, isn't she?" he said, coming over to the table. Simonne nodded. "She's okay," he said, his smile showing a missing tooth. "I like her. She's nice." He turned to his buddies and announced, "These guys know Mrs. Eccles. They're alright." Conflict averted, the beer continued to flow peacefully.

For the first time in her life, Sheila had an income that allowed her to spend some money on herself. After years of getting by with hand-me-down clothes from her American sisters and a few basic items she found on sale at Sears, she was now able to buy some new things for her wardrobe appropriate for a woman her age and in her job. Lean and fit, she didn't need to hide any imperfections and could look good in just about anything, but she wanted to look professional and tailored, no frills or ruffles, and needed clothes that were comfortable and easy to clean. She went directly to one of Peterborough's best ladies' wear stores, the one with a reputation for being very snooty and rather expensive.

"I hope you can help me," Sheila said to the elegant and well-coiffed saleslady who greeted her as she stepped through the door into the small shop. "I've just started a new job and I need some appropriate things to wear," she explained. If the sales person recognized that Sheila hadn't set foot in a store like this in a long time, she didn't show it, and neither did Sheila. It quickly became apparent she was a customer with good taste who recognized good value. An hour later, Sheila left with a few restrained business dresses, which suited her perfectly, and enough other items to be the basis of a good wardrobe. The store earned a loyal customer that day. Just because she hadn't been able to afford good clothes didn't mean Sheila'd given up on wanting to look and feel good.

By the time Sheila had finished college and started her job, the little pink and white house was almost paid for, much to Brownie's delight. He figured they could get by in retirement if they owned their home outright without a mortgage, and even had hopes of eventually starting his own pump repair business. Or he did, until the day Sheila went down to the basement to do the laundry and spied a rat scurrying away into the foundation. Screaming, she rushed, stumbling, back up the stairs. The basement was not well sealed, and had a partial gravel floor and a door to the outside. There were a lot of reasons a rat could be there, including the fact that Brownie's barn and his animals and feed were not far from the house. The "why" didn't matter.

"I will not live in a house where there's RATS! Rats bring disease! RATS! We could all be bitten and infected while we're sleeping! WE ARE MOVING!" Sheila ordered. Horrified, she refused to go down to the basement alone from that moment forward.

"Sheila, I caught the rat. It's gone. And there was only one." Brownie tried to reassure her. "And I will close up those places where it might come in."

"There's never only one!" Sheila insisted. "There'll be baby rats!" All Brownie's promises to fix the basement were to no avail. There was nothing he could do or say to convince her to stay in that house.

A couple of kilometres away, a small subdivision of new homes was being built just off the township road. Sheila saw this as opportunity knocking and went to talk to the builder. The most modest of the houses was a three bedroom bungalow, and while Brownie resisted moving at all, not wanting to give up his barn and his animals, he eventually came around to thinking it might be a compromise, a way to keep the peace. Purchasing the small bungalow would add only a couple of years to the mortgage and would placate Sheila, he reasoned.

She had bigger plans. Sheila had her eye on a larger split-level house, which cost more, but was definitely more impressive.

"I'll have to work a lot more years to pay it off," Brownie moaned. "Can't we just get the smaller place? Why do we need a big house at this stage in our lives?" But there was no talking Sheila out of it. With her new job and their two incomes, she was confident they could manage a bigger mortgage.

They moved in mid-summer 1970. Sheila's brand-new home still smelled of paint and new wood. It had hardwood floors, a new bronze stove and fridge, a second bathroom, and, for the first time, a shower. There was a dedicated laundry room with an automatic washer and dryer to replace the old wringer washer. Finally the pattern of moving downward in housing quality had been broken. It was a significant accomplishment and Sheila was proud. Her income made possible the custom-made drapes she chose for the bay window and the thick forest green area carpets.

Sheila gave a hundred percent to her job and worked hard to provide good service to her employer as well as her clients, but as the months turned into years, something began going wrong and she failed to see it, or she failed to pay attention to the brewing problems, or she thought they would go away. Until one day, in late 1971, when she came home from work and announced she had been fired.

"I've got something to tell you," she said that evening when supper was over. She was still sitting at the table while Scott and Holly were clearing up the dishes. Brownie had moved into the living room to watch TV. Sheila had been uncharacteristically quiet since she'd come home from work. "I was called into the manager's office today," she continued, " and the personnel director was there too." Brownie looked up, aware that something was about to happen. "I've been let go," she blurted.

"What do you mean you've been let go?" he said. "You've been fired? Why?" He came back to stand in the doorway to the kitchen. Holly and Scott stopped stacking the dirty plates and watched quietly.

"I don't really know," she said. "I don't have an answer to that. They simply told me I'm no longer required."

"There has to be a reason," Brownie said. "Did you do something wrong?"

"I don't know." Sheila's voice rose. "I thought I was doing a really good job." She stood up from the table and walked away.

If Sheila was ever given a clear reason for her dismissal, she didn't share it with her family. She said she didn't know for sure, or understand, what she was supposed to have done wrong, or not done at all, and wouldn't discuss it. Brownie silently wondered if there'd been a complaint from a welfare recipient, although that seemed unlikely. On the contrary, Sheila was so determined to help people that perhaps she wasn't turning down enough applicants. He then thought maybe she was telling her clients about their rights of appeal or giving advice on areas that conflicted with her job. Brownie knew she was far too honest to have cooked the books or benefitted herself in any way. He finally concluded this was a repeat of her experience at the training school and her long-past fight with the school board. Sheila was still trying to fix systems that didn't want to be fixed.

She packed up her desk, reeling in shock. It was the early 1970s and it was still possible to get fired from a municipal job without cause and without repercussions. She had worked for the city for less than three years.

Sheila took on battles and hadn't learned to take no for an answer if she thought she was right. She wanted to change the inequities she saw, right the wrongs, and fix unfairness. It was hard for her to understand her failure in light of all the positive feedback she had received and the hard work she had put into the job. And it made a devastating hole in the confidence she'd built through college and in the years after.

The financial ramifications were significant. There was no more second income in the family and no more company car at Sheila's disposal, no more pension plan. Eighteen months after they had purchased their new house and increased their mortgage, Sheila was again unemployed.

CHAPTER 19
A HOUSEWIFE AGAIN:
EARLY 1970's

The pleasure of jumping out of bed in the morning was gone, and along with it, Sheila's income and, more importantly, the sense of accomplishment it had represented. Gone too was the self-esteem from people valuing her advice and opinion. In place of the camaraderie and support of her coworkers, Sheila's daily companions became self doubt and worry.

She had lost far more than a job.

Early each workday morning, the house emptied, leaving Sheila on her own. *Why bother getting up? I'll just be in the way,* she thought, as she lay in bed listening to the rest of the family bustling around, getting ready for their day's activities. *I'll be one more person in the bathroom. When they're all gone I can get up and make my tea. I have nowhere to go anyway, and no reason to get out of bed.*

If Sheila needed the understanding and support from her family, she didn't ask for it. The kids were all too preoccupied with their own lives to pay much attention to how their mother felt. Brownie, as usual, stayed quietly in the background and waited things out. If anyone recognized how hurt and demeaned she felt, they ignored it.

"You'd better get another job soon," Simonne joked to Sheila early in the summer of 1972 as they were washing the dishes after dinner. Sheila turned and stared at her, momentarily speechless. "You're going to have a wedding to pay for." This was how Simonne announced she was getting married in a couple of months to her long time boyfriend Guy.

"Oh, how lovely!" Sheila said with a big smile, her shocked expression turning to joy. "When? Where? What shall we do?"

Then, she imparted her only advice about marriage. "You can't change him, you know," she said half jokingly, half serious and hopeful. Sheila's relationship with her prospective son-in-law had always had an undercurrent of tension and intellectual competition.

It was going to be the family's second wedding in a year. Randy had married his girlfriend Cathy at Thanksgiving the year before.

Sheila was far from a mother-of-the-bride tyrant, but she badly wanted to mark the occasion of her first daughter's wedding with a significant celebration. When she had been married in her army uniform at Ghent's city hall twenty-five years earlier, she had had no opportunity for a fancy dress or a family party, so she hoped this wedding would be a bit more of a splash. As all her suggestions and input were summarily rejected, she kept her calm. "I don't want a wedding dress!" Simonne insisted. "I don't want a sit down dinner!"

"But you need to make this a special event," Sheila kept patiently telling her. "You'll only do this once and you want to look back on it with pleasure." A compromise was finally reached for a big party at the Legion after a simple marriage ceremony in the local rural church. Sheila looked elegant and poised in the same tailored silver suit she had worn to Randy's wedding. Brownie sobbed quietly as he gave his eldest daughter away.

A few days later, when the excitement of the wedding was over and all the visiting guests had gone home, the bride and groom packed up their wedding presents and said their good-byes at the door. As always, Sheila followed them out to the driveway, chatting as they got into the car. As Guy put it in reverse and began backing out, Sheila was still bending down to talk to Simonne through the open passenger window, commenting on the events of the weekend and passing along advice. Once out on the street, Guy put the car in drive and began slowly to increase the speed.

"It was so lovely to see Aunt Agnes, wasn't it?" Sheila said, speaking more loudly over the engine noise. "I'm thrilled she could make it."

"Me too," replied Simonne.

"Now, did you pack all the gifts carefully? We don't want anything broken, do we? Should we have another look in the trunk to make sure nothing slides around?"

"It's fine." Guy continued to look straight ahead as he sped up a bit more.

"When do you think you'll be back?"

By this time they were moving along the road, Sheila trotting along the side of the car and trying to keep up. "Do drive carefully! Call us when you get there," she shouted. She finally gave up and stood on the side of the road, waving and blowing kisses until she could no longer see the car.

Barring pouring rain or a snowstorm, this was how Sheila ended every visit. She always had something left to say, protracted good-byes part of the joy she took in sharing a conversation.

It was hard to watch TV if Sheila happened to be in the same room. "Did you see this?" she commented to no one in particular, talking over the voices from the TV as she held up an article from the paper. Often there was little or no response beyond "uh huh" or a nod. Brownie had learned to sit silently through *Hockey Night in Canada*, missing the play-by-play commentary, while there was a one-sided dialogue from across the room.

Sheila was used to Brownie's wall of companionable silence, and she had long given up trying to get him to comment on current events or much else. When there were others in the house, though, her kids, their spouses and friends, she wanted to engage in a conversation, delighted to hear other people's ideas and opinions. Growing up in her family's small house in Coventry, there had rarely been moments when someone wasn't talking. She sought out the stimulation of a meaningful chat about almost anything. "What did you think of the new traffic light at the end of the street? I jolly well hope that stops the speeders!"

"Mmmhmmm," from Brownie. She found something interesting in almost any topic, except sports, despite the fact that her attempts to engage in a conversation were sometimes thwarted and dismissed. "I can't relax at your parents' house," Guy often complained to Simonne. "When your mother's around, everything has to be turned into a discussion."

Not everyone shared that impression. Sheila happened to be in the driveway the day that one of Simonne's professors pulled in to return an essay she'd written. "It's so nice to meet you," Sheila said, shaking his hand warmly. "You're originally from the Netherlands, aren't you?" she added. "What part?" From that simple question, the conversation smoothly moved on to the places they both knew and the impact of the war on his family when he was just a baby. Sheila and the professor leaned against his car in the afternoon sunshine and talked about places and events decades ago, when he was a child and she was a young woman. Her dark eyes sparkled and her face beamed. Instead of the ordinary, rather care-worn mother her family took for granted, Sheila became a bright intelligent woman, engaged, conversing on an equal footing with a well-educated academic. Without even a hint of flirting or pretending to find him fascinating, Sheila charmed this man twenty-some years her junior. It was clear that she was genuinely interested in what he had to say, and he was equally enjoying her company.

On a sunny autumn day later than year, driving into town, Sheila was lost in thought as she often was, and oblivious to how fast she was actually going. She always took great pride in her careful and safe driving skills learned during the war, and could manoeuvre Brownie's big old sedans with ease, long before power steering or brakes. She knew she was a good driver, so she treated the speed limits as if they were for other not-so-skilled folks. That is, she did until this day when she was caught in a speed trap going far in excess of the posted limit. The radar bleeped on the dashboard of the police cruiser as Sheila zoomed by. Lights flashing, the police car pulled out and followed her until she finally noticed and pulled over.

"Hello officer," she said politely, rolling down the car window and smiling. "Is there a road block ahead?"

"No, madam," he replied sternly. "You were speeding. Do you know how fast you were going?"

"I wasn't going fast!" she said, shocked. "This is the speed I always drive on this street."

He had clocked her well over the limit. Sheila had no experience with radar traps, and she was horrified that someone thought she was not driving properly. She was also highly suspicious that the device could in any way be accurate.

The police officer went back to his car, checked her driver's licence, and returned with a hefty ticket. She was far over any accepted wiggle room for speeders, driving at almost 100 km/hour in a 60 zone.

"What's this?" she challenged him, horrified. "I was a driver in the war, you know! Lorries, and ambulances, and I've been driving here in Canada since 1946!" She didn't point out that was likely before the young officer was born. He looked at her, the small, indignant lady with the crisp English accent, the heavy foot, and the greying hair. He said nothing, but held the ticket out until she took it.

"I have a perfect driving record," she lectured him. "I HAVEN'T A BLEMISH!"

He looked at her for a moment. "Well, you do now," he retorted dryly, returned to his cruiser and drove off.

When Sheila got home later that afternoon and told the story, indignantly repeating again, "I HAVEN'T A BLEMISH!" she was greeted with hoots and guffaws of derision. "You've just been lucky so far," Brownie said, shaking his head and chuckling. "I always told you that you have a lead foot." If she had been expecting some supportive commiserating about the unfairness of the radar trap, she was mistaken. It was clear to Brownie and the rest of the family that Sheila's ticket was long overdue. "Just pay it and shut up," they advised, but of course, that was not going to happen. Sheila had never accepted the adage that you can't fight city hall, and she proceeded to do exactly that. After hours of research into the science behind radar speed traps, she prepared her defence and scheduled an appearance in court, armed with righteous indignation and bolstered with newspaper clippings about other cases.

The unfortunate young police officer was required to testify. On the witness stand, she grilled him about the calibration of his radar devise, his training, and his record of charging drivers. "How often do you issue a ticket rather than a warning?" Sheila asked. "Is this ratio higher than other officers?"

"I don't know," he fumbled.

"The reviews of radar accuracy conclude that it's in error up to 20% of the time, and if the police car is moving the error rate goes up to 30%. Were you aware of that?"

"Uhm, no, I guess I wasn't."

"The roads were clear and dry that day, weren't they?" she continued. "Were there other cars on the road at the time?"

"No," he replied.

"And was I in any way exhibiting a threat to cause an accident?" she followed up.

"No."

The magistrate looked on, impressed and amused. At the conclusion, he concurred with Sheila's points about the weaknesses of radar, and reduced the offence to a more reasonable and affordable ticket. "Well done Mrs. Eccles," he congratulated her. "I've seen lawyers who couldn't do as good a job as you did today." The now-subdued officer stopped her in the courthouse hall to shake her hand as she was leaving, lesson learned never to underestimate a determined woman.

Sheila's driving record remained blemish free, and in the fall of 1974, she was offered a job at the Cobourg Jail as a correctional officer, a "matron," as the position was then called. It meant she would need to drive more than fifty kilometres each way to the jail, in all kinds of weather, early mornings and late nights for various shifts. She jumped at the opportunity. The driving was a no-brainer. It gave her lots of time to think each way and to listen to CBC on the car radio. The position was only part-time and on-call, managing the women offenders who arrived on short notice, but she had hope that it might evolve into something bigger. She was just short of her fifty-sixth birthday, a time when many people would be looking ahead to retirement. For Sheila, it was an exciting new beginning.

Ironically this was a similar job with the same government department that had asked her to resign many years earlier from the Lindsay Girls Training School. Happily, it was also the point where Sheila finally broke her pattern of getting fired. This time, if she made suggestions, she did it in an appropriate way. She had learned not to try to change everything. Her work reviews were exemplary and her positive interactions with her fellow staff members as well as the inmates was a point of pride for her. In November 1974, just months after she'd been on the job, she received a written commendation from the jail's superintendent.

Thank you for the competent manner in which you handled a crisis in the Cobourg Jail. It is a pleasure to have people like yourself who display the appropriate reactions under crisis conditions.

Sheila carefully put the Superintendent's little note in a box with her other keepsakes and said nothing to the family about it. *It's nice to be appreciated and valued,* she thought. *I feel useful when I'm in jail, silly as that sounds.* She volunteered very little information about her job unless asked, but it was clear that she was happy.

Sheila held that job for almost eight years until 1982, faithfully driving the long distance to Cobourg when she was called in to work and always on time. When finally her contract couldn't be renewed, it was not because of the quality of her work or because she was sixty-three, but because the Cobourg Jail was no longer accepting female inmates. When Sheila asked to be moved over to a position on the men's side, she was told it couldn't be done. Women officers working with male offenders was a very new and not widely accepted idea. That barrier was finally broken a few years later.

In the reference letter on her departure, Sheila was described as "*a diligent, punctual and trustworthy employee who executed her duties as a correctional officer in an intelligent, compassionate manner.*" That positive assessment was almost verbatim a repeat of her military discharge four decades earlier.

Sheila and Brownie at Simonne's wedding, September 1972

CHAPTER 20
FROM MAYHEM TO PEACE:
1972 TO 1976

From feminism to gay rights, from student protests to prison rioting, the early 1970s witnessed social conflict around the globe. Even in the smaller world of Sheila's family no one was immune from challenge and change.

A new normal had settled over the household after Simonne's wedding on Labour Day 1972. There were now only two kids left at home. Sixteen-year-old Scott and Holly were still in high school, and those last teenage years before the twins left home should have been peaceful and easy ones for Sheila. Now in her early fifties with two married kids living away, she expected peace at home.

Scott had always been the adventurer who fell out of trees and banged his head and may have had childhood concussions. When he was about seven or eight, Sheila often woke up in the night to find him sleepwalking. She insisted to the family doctor that this was not normal, and pushed for answers until Scott was eventually referred to a specialist at SickKids Hospital in Toronto. Sheila turned the trip into an adventure for him, a special day out with his mom and dad, and she avoided any hint to her little boy that there might be something wrong with him.

Nothing was ever resolved, nothing abnormal found, and no diagnosis made. The sleep walking eventually just stopped, and Scott continued to be a likeable, curious, active little boy.

In high school, Scott's gregariousness and adventure seeking made him very attractive to the kids who pushed the limits. More and more he found himself stretched between the solid family life he had at home—a mother who expected him to do well academically and move on to post second-ary education and a father with whom he shared so many interests—versus acceptance from the "bad kids." It was a lot more fun and a lot easier to break the rules than to try to focus on classes, and more and more, Scott drifted to the dark side.

In 1973, he was busted at a school dance with a joint in his hand. Two plainclothes RCMP officers grabbed him outside the school that night as if they'd been waiting especially for Scott, and charged him with possession. Instead of sending him home, the officers let him go back into the school, where he was hailed as an instant hero by his buddies, moving straight to the inner circle of the bad kids and a downward spiral of more acting out. Although he was an immature seventeen-year-old, under the law at that time, he was no longer a juvenile offender but an adult, and he faced stiffer penal-ties for all his crimes.

Soon after, Scott accepted a dare to steal some stereo equipment from the school's music room, and was caught. He wasn't charged, but he was expelled, and responded by riding his motorcycle through the halls of the school. It was a pretty clear middle finger to authority.

Sheila was terrified. Her heart was breaking and she was sick with worry, but all of her confrontations and nagging couldn't change his behaviour. She was at her wits' end and so was Brownie, unable to verbalize how he felt or to say the things he wanted to say to Scott. Where Sheila raged, Brownie closed up and silently despaired.

On the day Scott went to court, Sheila and Brownie were in the visitors seats to watch the proceedings. Sheila sat rigid on the wooden bench, barely able to catch her breath, feeling as if she'd been punched in the chest. Brownie had his head down, his hands clenched by his sides and his jaw tight. Neither of them had ever imagined they would see one of their children in the prisoner's box.

It took only a few minutes for Scott to plead guilty and be sentenced to adult probation. As they watched him leave the courtroom Sheila wanted to scream, *He's only a boy!* The local newspaper reported the conviction in the criminal court section, along with the names of other offenders Sheila knew from her days as a welfare worker. There was only one Eccles listed in the local phone book, only one family by that name in the whole area. Anyone who knew Brownie from the Co-op knew Scott had to be his son.

On the day Sheila decided to search Scott's room, not long after his day in court, she found, as she expected, more drugs. "Brownie!" she screamed as she ran downstairs to the kitchen with the evidence. "Look at what Scott had hidden in his clothes! I can't believe he is still this stupid." She was frantic. "We can't let this go on! I won't have this in our house! I'm calling the RCMP to come and get this."

Sheila reached for the phone hanging on the kitchen wall and Brownie grabbed it from her hand. "No, Sheila!" he yelled. He continued more quietly, "No, Sheila. You can't do this. I won't let you do this to Scott." She continued to try to pull the phone away from him, but Brownie held on. "No, Sheila! We won't turn in our own son." They stood in the small kitchen, nose to nose, struggling for the phone, breathing hard in anger and anxiety until finally Sheila let go. "But we'll talk to him as soon as he comes home," she insisted.

"Yes," Brownie nodded, and gently put the phone back on its hook.

Sheila and Brownie were waiting in the kitchen when Scott came home, the big bag of weed she'd discovered sitting on the table between them. "How do you explain this?" Sheila demanded. "You promised you were finished with drugs!" Panicking, sick with fear and shame, Scott exploded. "WHY DON'T YOU JUST FUCK OFF AND LEAVE ME ALONE!" he shouted.

Brownie jumped up from his chair, knocking it to the floor with a loud bang, grabbed Scott roughly by the collar, and shoved him back. "DON'T YOU *EVER* TALK TO YOUR MOTHER LIKE THAT!" he yelled. Shocked to be on the receiving end of Brownie's so rarely viewed anger, Scott backed down. "I'm sorry," he said, and meant it. Sorry that he had sworn at his mother, but even sorrier that he'd caused such heartache to the father he respected more than anything.

Brownie was always non-committal, avoiding conflict, not wanting to rock the boat. But back him against the wall, and he came out swinging. Despite his hatred of violence, he would have punched Scott to protect Sheila, and would have hated himself for it.

It was all such a mess.

Sheila was a stickler for following the rules, except perhaps speed limits and occasionally breaking into an empty house. She liked schedules and structure, like she'd had in the military. She established set bedtimes for her children and expected good table manners. She couldn't stand chaos, but she was not reticent to step outside the lines if she thought she could affect a needed change. She was willing to stand up to a conservative rural school board or to voice an unpopular opinion in a letter to the editor. She lost her job for being a whistleblower. She was prepared to do whatever she could to turn Scott around, and with her great respect for law and order, she naïvely thought the police would help her. This time, instead of standing back, Brownie had stepped in to stop her from making a bad situation worse. He just wanted to hold his family close and protect them from harm and pain.

A few weeks later, Brownie and Scott made a road trip to the farm in Mount Forest. It was a chance for the two of them to reclaim some of their lost father-son closeness, and an effort on Brownie's part to get Scott away from his peers, and maybe ease the tension with Sheila, for at least a weekend. Scott's grandfather, the man he was named after, greeted him, unsmiling. "Oh, you're here," he said to his young namesake. "I thought you were in jail." Three generations of men stood on the farmhouse porch; no one moved, the tension palpable. Scott, humiliated, tried to brazenly laugh it off.

Brownie hung his head in front of his father, ashamed for both of them, but relieved that Sheila wasn't there to witness it.

In their different ways, Sheila and Brownie both understood the restlessness and confusion Scott was experiencing.

"You aren't always going to feel this way," Sheila told Scott one day in a quiet and calm moment some weeks after their battle over his bag of weed. The two of them were having lunch in the kitchen, and she was treading carefully around the topic of his plans for the future now that he was no longer in school. Behind her words, her message to Scott was not to give up on himself. She too had been disappointed and stung a few times by life, had been confused and unsure, but had picked herself up and moved on. It became a mantra that resonated with Scott for the rest of his life, and one he passed on again and again to troubled kids in his adult career as a boxing coach.

Meanwhile, as all of the family drama was swirling around her, Holly quietly carried on. She was the shy one of the family, sensitive, and on the surface, not as confident as Scott. She was an introvert, but when pushed, stubborn. Holly lived in the same house and attended the same high school as her twin brother, but moved in an entirely different direction. When he was expelled, she graduated. As Sheila and Brownie's attention was focused on Scott out of necessity, his twin sister became more and more independent and self-reliant.

Holly was eighteen in 1974 when she started the two-year forest technician program at Fleming College, one of only a handful of women in a program that had traditionally been all male. At the end of her first year, she accepted a summer job with the Ministry of Natural Resources in Cochrane, the first time girls were hired to work in the bush. She didn't exactly know where Cochrane was, aside from somewhere in northern Ontario, until she pulled a roadmap out to find it. It was a twelve-hour train ride. With fifty dollars in her pocket, borrowed from Brownie, and one backpack of clothes, she made the trip with a classmate she barely knew. They weren't even sure they had a place to live when they got there. It was another reminder of Sheila's bike ride to Bournemouth for her first job, forty years earlier. It was a giant leap of faith for Sheila to let her shy and gentle youngest child leave home for the unknown woods of northern Ontario.

Holly didn't come back. By the time September rolled around, she had decided she wasn't returning to school to finish her course. She was in love with her supervisor Andy, and Cochrane was the only place she wanted to be, with him. Sheila was disappointed and very concerned that Holly wasn't going to finish her education, but more importantly, she was giving it up for what Sheila figured was going to be a short-term romance. Brownie was sad his little girl wasn't coming home. Both were worried about their sweet, innocent daughter.

When Sheila and Brownie decided to make the long drive to Cochrane to pay a surprise visit, it was Sheila who got the biggest shock. Holly and Andy were living together. It was the middle 70s and attitudes about premarital sex and cohabiting had changed drastically since Sheila's youth as the impact of feminism had risen, and birth control was easily available. Nonetheless, Sheila, despite her forward thinking, was aghast.

"We can't allow her to live like this!" she ranted to Brownie as she paced their motel room. "This is just not right. She barely knows this man."

"No, Sheila. Leave her be." Brownie sat on the end of the bed and watched as she marched back and forth across the worn carpet. "No, Sheila."

"Pack your things." Sheila insisted to Holly back at the apartment she was sharing with Andy, hoping if she couldn't convince Brownie she could at least bully Holly into returning. "You're coming home with us." Equally determined and stubborn, Holly resisted. "No, Mom. I'm staying here."

"No, Sheila," Brownie repeated, again and again that weekend. "No, Sheila. She's a smart girl and she has to figure this out on her own. When she wants to come home, she will."

It took the entire weekend for Sheila to finally accept that she wasn't going to break down Brownie and Holly's resistance and she wasn't going to bring Holly back. They returned to Peterborough without her. It was a long and tense drive as Sheila seethed in the passenger seat.

Sheila had had her own whirlwind wartime romance, and had seen lots of other couples move in together. Scott was "living in sin" with his girlfriend and she took this in stride, but her attitude was entirely different when it came to Holly. Sheila and Brownie had never voiced anything derogatory about common-law relationships, apart from a raised eyebrow or a reference to the woman as "Mrs. John" instead of "Mrs. Smith," as if she didn't merit the husband's last name. Sheila's strong resistance to Holly's living situation didn't fit with her otherwise modern views.

She insisted Holly must get married. She had lost the battle about leaving Holly in Cochrane, but intended to control how she lived her life there. "If you're going to live with Andy," she told Holly on the phone repeatedly, "you should be married. Make the commitment. Make it official and legal. Protect your rights. Think about your future children." She nagged relentlessly until Holly finally gave up resisting and gave in to what her mother wanted. Much like Brownie, Holly preferred peace over confrontation. Sheila then moved on to the wedding dress, adamant that Holly couldn't wear white at her wedding, as if engaging in pre-marital sex somehow made her less worthy. Ultimately, Holly yielded on that issue too.

Holly stayed in northern Ontario all her life, and remained married to Andy. He quickly became Sheila's favorite son in-law. They often sat for hours late into the night, engaged in long conversations, enjoying shots of whiskey and each other's point of view. It was Andy's Indigenous heritage and stories of his family that sparked her interest in pursuing Native Studies in later years.

About that time, Scott left for the boom of Calgary and the lure of well-paying construction jobs. Brownie had helped him fix up a decrepit old van just to get around Peterborough, and one day, on a whim, Scott packed it up and drove it all the way out west, taking his troubles with him.

In the short space of just a few years, all four kids were gone, the dramas more or less over, the unused bedrooms getting dusty. The house became very quiet, and the phone rang much less frequently. It was just Sheila and Brownie again, no buffer of teenagers coming and going, no lively dinner time conversations of what had happened that day, no slammed doors. Aside from the two months between Sheila's arrival in Canada and Randy's birth, for the first time in their married life, there were no children's voices in their home. It was the first time in almost thirty years, since May of 1946, that they had just each other for company.

Now what?

Brownie at work, early 1970s.

CHAPTER 21
THE EMPTY NEST:
1970's TO 80's

"Should I have told you what it was like?" Sheila asked.

She was sitting carefully on the side of Simonne's hospital bed, holding her hand, just hours after Simonne had given birth to her first child. She was almost apologetic and a little embarrassed, referring to the actual delivery process. Simonne laughed and shook her head. "No Mom, I did prenatal classes and I was pretty well prepared." They had never talked about pregnancy in any detail, and Sheila hadn't offered any suggestions other than general references to health. Properly English, she still referred to breasts as bosoms and a uterus as a womb and, in typical British fashion, employed euphemisms to describe very personal medical parts "down there." She had never talked with her daughters about the delivery of any of her own children, about breastfeeding, or about anything associated with the messier parts of giving birth.

Sheila and Brownie had been up at dawn to make the drive to Kingston as soon as they got the phone call, and burst into the hospital room just hours after their first grandson Michael was born in September 1976. Brownie grinned from ear to ear with that same look of wonder he had when he announced the birth of the twins. He immediately went to the bassinette and picked up the baby, cooing. Unlike Sheila, Brownie was not uncomfortable talking about births. He'd seen lots of them on the farm. He was a person that dogs and children instinctively go to, and he was totally at ease caring for babies and changing diapers.

Over the next few years more grandchildren followed, and by the time all was said and done, there were nine in total, plus two step-grandchildren. Sheila maintained a non-interference strategy, keeping her worries and anything other than general observations to herself unless asked, and letting her adult children move in their own child-rearing directions. As a result, the joy of family get-togethers was never tainted by criticism or judgment. When everyone could gather for Christmas or for summer visits at the house in Peterborough, it was a happy time, little cousins seeing each other again with their aunts and uncles and grandparents.

Sheila's gifts to the grandkids were always modest but practical and well thought out. Books, crayon sets, and educational puzzles topped her list. As the grandkids got older, she took them on afternoons to explore the nearby pioneer village in Lang or the Indigenous petroglyph cave carvings. She had rarely played games with her own children and didn't with her grandchildren either, but she planted ideas and fed imaginations. When grandma Sheila whispered in a child's ear, "there are fairies at the bottom of the garden," her grandchildren believed her.

Holly was visiting from Cochrane one summer and all the young grandkids were outside playing "Cowboys and Indians." Through the open kitchen window, Sheila could overhear them shouting as they chased each other across the lawn and around the house. "Get the Indians! Shoot the Indians!" they called, every one of them a cowboy chasing a "savage." Sheila stepped out the back door and gathered them together around her. "Why do you want to shoot the Indians?" she asked seriously, arms folded over her chest, looking at each child. Her grandchildren stood quietly for a moment, considering the question, no one really knowing why. It was what they saw on TV. "Didn't you know your daddy is an Indian man?" she asked Holly's son Colin. His eyes widened. "And your other grandmother in Cochrane is too?" The grandkids didn't say anything for a moment as the notion took hold. But soon, Colin shouted, "Let's chase the cowboys!" and the game quickly reversed. Even in play, Sheila found room for a lesson in equality.

Through the 60s and early 70s Sheila and Brownie had stuck pretty close to home. There were no actual vacations and only a few road trips and overnight stays, occasional visits to Brownie's family or to see Randy in Burlington, and a few trips north to Cochrane to see Holly or to Kingston to visit Simonne. They hadn't visited Sheila's family in the USA for a long time.

Sheila liked to drive, but was far from relaxed when she wasn't in the driver's seat. Even from the passenger side she kept her eyes fixed on the road and her right foot ready to hit the brake pedal that wasn't there. Each of her kids had had the experience of piping up from the backseat, "Mom, look at that!" as they passed something interesting on the side of the road. "I can't look. I'm driving!" she always shot back, even though she was in the passenger seat. The only time she and Brownie drove over the long in-need-of-repair causeway bridge at Rouse's Point, crossing Lake Champlain to get from New York State to Vermont and on to her sisters in New Hampshire, Sheila was terrified. When she couldn't talk Brownie into turning around and taking the long way around the lake, she threatened to get out of the car and walk across the bridge. Finally, with no other option, she made the crossing in the car with her window open and her door slightly ajar in case they went into the water and she had to make a hasty swim to safety. Brownie took a different route the next time.

Despite Sheila's white knuckles, the road trips continued. She was always enthusiastic about the idea of travel and in particular loved to see her American siblings. Her passenger jitters were well known to her older sisters and became a source of their fun. On their day-trips to antique and second-hand stores, with Sheila as a passenger, they tortured her with fast cornering and sudden braking, much to Brownie's amusement and the sisters' gales of laughter. The temptation to tease their younger sister hadn't decreased despite their grey hair.

Sheila's opportunity to travel even further came as a surprise in late 1980.

"We're moving to Alberta," Simonne told Sheila and Brownie in a phone call one Sunday afternoon that fall. It was a *fait accompli*, no discussion and no consultation in advance. "You're going where?" Sheila said, surprised. "Why? When will we ever get to see you?"

"I guess you're going to have to get on an airplane at last," Simonne joked. "Edmonton is two thousand miles away and I doubt you'll want to drive."

With Holly's children a full day away in Cochrane, and Randy's children hours away in Burlington, Sheila and Brownie's only local grandchildren were Scott's. They were not the kind of grandparents who helicoptered over the grandkids, but they were very disappointed to have them spread so far away. Sheila understood the excitement of change, and the lure of adventure. She'd been willingly uprooted throughout the war, and she'd made a life-changing decision to come to Canada, leaving her parents and home behind. While moving to Alberta was not nearly so dramatic, Sheila knew it would have a massive impact on Simonne's day-to-day life and on her children, and that Simonne was risking potential loneliness and isolation, at least initially. She kept those thoughts to herself.

Sheila's travel experience was restricted to trains and ships, where she generally got very seasick, and cars, where she was a very nervous passenger. If she wanted to visit her daughter and grandchildren, she was going to have to fly to Edmonton, and perhaps convince Brownie to come with her. That seemed unlikely. Brownie was always a reluctant traveller, except when he could drive to visit family. His war years had provided him with enough travel for a lifetime. All that aside, Sheila and Brownie decided they were going to Alberta.

They arrived at Edmonton International Airport on a sunny summer day in 1983, none the worse for wear, coming briskly through the arrivals gate, grins on their faces and suitcases in hand. "How was your trip?" Simonne asked, hugging each one in turn. "Did you have any trouble figuring out all the check in procedures?"

"It was fine," Brownie said, as if to imply she had underestimated their abilities. "There were lovely flight attendants who helped us," Sheila added, "It was all rather exciting, and I felt very high class and modern!"

Reticent as Brownie always was to tell war stories, he had never mentioned to his kids that he had a cousin, Arthur Brown, living not far from Simonne in Edmonton, and he wanted to reconnect with him. The cousins had been pals as farm kids in Mount Forest before the war, and when Brownie was torpedoed in the Mediterranean, Arthur was one of the first people to pull him ashore onto the beach in Sicily. The two soldiers hadn't even known where the other one was at the time until they accidentally met up on that war-time beach, and in the intervening forty years, they had rarely seen each other. They were overdue for a reunion.

"Arthur's taking me out to the oil rigs where he worked, somewhere closer to the mountains," Brownie said, the morning after they had arrived. "I'm not sure where it is or how far."

"Oh how lovely," Sheila encouraged him. "You've never seen the Rockies before and you'll have a wonderful time. You two need a chance to catch up and get to know each other again." She knew the Italy beach story and was quite happy to see Brownie enjoying this old family connection, content to stay back and relax with her grandkids.

Dinnertime came and went without Brownie, and Simonne began to worry about her father. He hadn't left a phone number or even anything specific about where he was going to be, or how long he'd be gone. He hadn't packed any clothes or taken his tooth brush. "Where is he?" she asked, unrealistically expecting he would have been back by then. "What if he's lost on the side of the road somewhere? Or stuck in the mountains? He doesn't know anything about Alberta." As the hours ticked away, her concern changed to annoyance.

"Stop worrying," Sheila the worrier said, uncharacteristically. "He's fine. Let your father have some fun. He deserves it. He'll be home when he's ready."

Brownie got back late the next day, tired, happy and totally unconcerned that anyone might have wondered where he was all night. Sheila greeted him with a smile and "I hope you had a wonderful visit. Let's hear about your adventures."

They stayed for a week, one of the longest visits Sheila and Brownie had ever spent in the home of one of their children. Sheila was at ease, relaxed and enjoying just being there. *How does a working mother manage to get all this done?* she wondered, watching her daughter's domestic routines unfold. *I don't know if I could have done all this.*

She took her grandchildren to the park, giving them her full attention, and sat on the couch quietly reading them stories. The week passed quickly, the sunny days unclouded by any conflict. It was a pleasant reminder of Sheila's child-rearing years, enjoying tea and cookies on quiet summer afternoons in Rothsay with her kids .

Although Sheila made only one visit to Alberta, she was a constant presence through the thread of her letters. She wrote to Simonne often, as she did to Holly, and to Scott when he lived in Calgary, and as she had always done with her brothers and sisters. Her letters were newsy and conversational, sometimes composed over several days, with newspaper clippings and old recipes often included. *Here's Amy's raisin pudding,* she wrote. *It used to be one of your favorites.* Another time she included "Grandma Eccles' Green Tomato Relish," quickly scribbled on a scrap of stained notepaper. She gave updates about things happening in Brownie's life as well as the rest of the family and the neighbours. She asked questions about her grandchildren and commented on artwork and scribblings they had sent. Once in a while, she added a bit of folksy philosophy when she had been feeling particularly nostalgic or whimsical.

She wrote prolifically, but not all of Sheila's letters got mailed. In one of the many boxes of unsorted pictures and documents she left behind, one envelope stood out. It was a grassy shade of green, with a stamp as if it was just waiting to be dropped into the mailbox. It had never been posted. Inside were two letters from Sheila to Simonne, one dated simply March '86, and the other April.

I have as usual letters here I never mail to you. I re-read the next morning and decide I am weird—ha ha! I wish I had learnt to do better for you all when I was younger. You were all lovely kids.

Don't be afraid to say during life "Hey God, thanks a lot, it was a good day." I do all the time. He/she has been good to me, not in everything, but in most. Love each other, count your blessings, and be happy.

She had written some private thoughts, and then, embarrassed by her own sentimentality, had thrown the envelope in a drawer and decided not to send it. Simonne found it thirty years later, as if their conversation continued across the decades.

When she almost shared those feelings, Sheila could not have known that her blessings were soon to be numbered.

Sheila with sisters Agnes (centre) and Kathleen (right). November 1986

CHAPTER 22
HELLO AGAIN CANCER: 1987

"I've enrolled at Trent University," Sheila had announced to Brownie back in the summer of 1979.

He looked up from the armchair where he was beginning to doze. He said nothing but raised his eyebrows in a question. "I know there won't be a wonderful job at the end of the rainbow," she quickly added before he could comment, "and maybe I won't even get far enough for a B.A., but I'm going to try."

Brownie nodded. "Okay," he said, knowing if Sheila was happy and busy he could be happy too. He had hobbies, and hers was going to be Trent University. Their live could move along peacefully, he hoped, and he wouldn't need to adjust in any major way.

The desire to earn a university degree had been growing in Sheila for many years, and now, with time on her hands, she believed it was actually achievable. Her ambition was greater than just seeing the letters B.A. after her name. She was hungry for the stimulation of learning, of discussing ideas and theories, of pushing herself to think beyond her everyday world. She had observed Simonne's university years from the sidelines with enthusiasm and support, and a bit of envy, and felt it was now possible that she herself could participate in a similar experience. In small part, she was encouraged because the province had introduced a program to waive tuition fees for citizens aged sixty and over. She had reached that threshold a few months earlier, so cost was no longer a barrier. She had been cancer free for many years, was healthy and energetic, and she knew she could manage part-time courses without giving up her occasional jail shifts.

It was no surprise she was majoring in Aboriginal Studies.

Eight years later, by the spring of 1987, Sheila could almost taste her degree, and she was pleased with the growing number of credits under her belt. She had squeaked by with a shaky D in a challenging third year Anthropology course, "Art of the Americas," and had done slightly better in "Politics and Legal Anthropology" with a solid C. She wasn't in the top half of her class as she'd been at community college in the 1960s, but she had a smattering of Bs to balance the lower grades, and if she were being marked on enthusiasm and hard work she would have merited an A plus.

When Sheila registered for the last two courses she needed, she couldn't have known that a bigger challenge was going to literally take over her life.

With her courses finished for the spring semester and her passing grades in her pocket, Sheila and Brownie made a long overdue trip to Cochrane to visit Holly. Sheila was looking forward to spending some time with her young grandchildren and was trying to ignore the health issue that been plaguing her over the past while. She was having a lot of difficulty swallowing and eating, and she was losing weight from her already thin body. She often choked, and even drinking her favorite tea had become a challenge.

At Stedman's lunch bar in Cochrane, Holly was looking forward to a relaxed meal with Sheila, and a little mother/daughter bonding time, but after Sheila's first bite, she stood up abruptly and pushed her chair back from the table. "Not well," she mumbled and rushed between the other tables to the washroom. Holly waited uncomfortably, worrying as time passed and Sheila hadn't returned. Finally, she went to check. "Are you okay Mom?" she asked as she knocked on the door to the ladies' room.

"Yes, sorry, I'm coming. Something went down the wrong way." Sheila finally came back to the table but didn't touch her lunch.

Over the next few days Holly watched as Sheila carefully sipped her drinks but avoided eating. She pushed her food to one side of the plate and made excuses. "I'm just tired I think. You've made lovely meals Holly, but I don't seem to be hungry." She brushed off all Holly's questions and concerns. Unknown to Holly, a week or so earlier Simonne had made the same observations. "You should mention that choking on your next visit to the doctor," Simonne had told Sheila. "That shouldn't be happening."

"Yes, I will," Sheila had agreed, and then changed the subject.

The symptoms of cancer of the esophagus are not pleasant. Swallowing is difficult, with a sensation that food is stuck part way, or it actually is. This leads to weight loss, and hoarseness, a chronic cough, and even chest pain, and there can be related gastrointestinal issues. Sheila didn't know her actual diagnosis when she visited Holly, but she knew something was seriously wrong and she was afraid. As usual, she avoided discussing her health issues with anyone in the family, including Brownie.

The night before Sheila's second cancer operation was eerily a repeat of the night before her breast surgery twenty years earlier. "It's just a routine procedure," she told Brownie when she asked him to drop her off at the hospital. As always, he said okay, and didn't press her for more details. There wasn't a reason for him to doubt her. She had said that before in recent years when having various routine GYN procedures. She didn't say the word cancer or explain that she was having surgery. She didn't warn him that esophageal cancer is very serious, and that the prognosis is poor. She kept those facts strictly to herself, as if she was willfully ignoring the reality of her illness, or she was hoping for a miracle.

Holly was in Peterborough for her annual summer visit when Sheila's surgery was scheduled, so she went with Brownie to drop her mother at the hospital. After she'd been checked in, Brownie and Holly waited in Sheila's hospital room to say goodnight to her. She had been taken to another floor for some last minute check, and a long time went by before she returned. "The nurse left me sitting in a room, forgotten!" she complained angrily when she was finally brought back, upset and frightened. "Is this the quality of treatment I can expect tomorrow?" Sheila railed to them. "How can they misplace a patient?"

"We'd better leave you now to rest, and we'll pick you up tomorrow," Brownie said, trying to get out of the way of her anger. "And good luck!" Holly added with a smile, although they weren't sure what they were wishing luck about. They were walking down the hall towards the elevator when a nurse came after them. "Please wait. I need to talk to you," she said, leading them to chairs in the visitor room. "I don't think Mrs. Eccles has told you everything, has she?" They looked at her, confused. "Do you know she's gravely ill?" she added kindly, touching Brownie's hand. "Your wife has cancer and her operation tomorrow morning is very serious. *If* she survives the surgery, she'll go to the Intensive Care Unit for a few days at least." Holly and Brownie sat, speechless and shocked. They didn't know what to say.

"I know this is difficult for you. Go home and try not to worry," the nurse said. "Stay by your phone. I'm on duty tomorrow, and I promise I'll call you with updates".

Brownie had known none of this but he was not surprised. He had been afraid something was wrong for quite a while, and he knew Sheila was likely in denial and hoping for the best in order to save her family from reality. The nurse's comments were more of a shock for Holly. "I feel like Mom has left me in the dark again, like when I was child," she said to Brownie, in tears as they were driving away. "Same as when she went to the hospital and had a breast removed and I didn't understand anything.

"Why does she always leave us out?" Holly cried. "I would have hugged her back there, and told her not to be scared. I could have tried to comfort her! She needed it, and so do I. Oh Dad, I didn't get to say I love you." Brownie blinked back his own tears and silently drove home.

As she'd promised to do, the nurse called every hour when Sheila finally came out of her long surgery the next day. "She made it this far," she reported.

She called again later, saying, "She made it through another couple of hours." There was no point in going to the hospital because they weren't allowed to see her yet. While they waited at home all that day, Brownie worked on repairing his old truck in the backyard to keep his mind and hands busy. Holly coped as she always did: by cooking, making jam from the fruit on Sheila's currant bushes. Occupied with their own lives, Randy, Scott and Simonne had no real understanding of what was actually going on, and that was how Sheila had intended it.

When they were finally able to visit her, Brownie and Holly were totally unprepared for what they saw. Sheila's face had ballooned beyond recognition. There were tubes and machines attached to her, humming and whirring as they monitored her body functions. Only her O'Carroll eyes looked the same, a tiny piece of Sheila behind all the medical paraphernalia.

Holly stood terrified and shaking as she looked at Sheila sedated and secured in the ICU bed, barely containing her emotions until she could get out of the hospital. She burst into tears as soon as she got to the parking lot. "Oh Dad," she sobbed. "Oh Dad!"

"There's no use crying," was all he said. He was just as worried as Holly, but he bottled it inside. He slumped heavily into the driver's seat and sat with his head down, unspeaking for a moment before starting the car.

Sheila remained in the ICU for several days, unable to speak for the tubes down her throat and the damage from her surgery. As the sedation was reduced, she became more alert and the nurses gave her a clipboard and pen so she could communicate in a basic way. Holly tried to cheer her with snippets of information about home. "While you've been in here, I picked the currants from your garden and made jam. You're going to love it. It turned out great." Sheila nodded and let go of Holly's hand to pick up her clipboard. She shakily wrote, "Vitamin C", underlining it for emphasis.

Simonne was the last of Sheila's children to visit her in hospital. "Wait until she feels better," Brownie had told her several times during his telephone updates. "She won't even know you're here." When she finally went to visit, Sheila had been moved to a regular hospital room, and her face lit up with a beautiful smile when Simonne walked in. Sheila reached out for her hand. "I'm so happy to see you. How are your kiddies doing with all the renovations going on in your house?" Sheila whispered in her scratchy voice. "It must be so hard while you're both trying to go to work and do so many other things."

"That's why I wasn't here sooner," Simonne explained, "I'm sorry. I didn't realize what you were going through." Sheila brushed off any discussion of her surgery. "I wouldn't have known if you'd been here or not." She kept her eyes on Simonne's and quickly changed the subject. "Now tell me about your house." Sheila treated this medical episode as one-and-done, and she was moving forward.

Although Sheila didn't want attention and fussing from her children, she did have expectations of the hospital staff. Frustrated by her inability to communicate well, she was not an easy patient. Despite her weak voice, she asked the nurses for explanations of each procedure, leaving them with the impression she was demanding and difficult, while she felt she was being brushed off. One nurse misinterpreted this as a sense of entitlement. Perhaps Sheila had her proper-dignified-English-lady persona on. Maybe she buzzed the buzzer one time too many, or asked for something trivial like a cup of tea from an overworked staff member. Whatever it was, it was too much for this particular nurse. "Your attitude is why your kids don't come to visit you!" the nurse snapped at her. "Because you are too damn demanding."

That nurse suddenly found herself challenged by a very feisty sixty-eight-year-old patient. "I want to speak to the head nurse about you!" Sheila croaked, shaking her finger inches from the nurse's nose.

"I *am* the Head Nurse," the nurse replied, now taken aback. This was a side of the patient she hadn't seen before.

"I am a war veteran, and I deserve more respect from you!" Sheila said with as much dignity and strength as she could muster from her damaged voice. She had stood up to lots of disrespect in her life, and wasn't about to be bullied regardless of the circumstances. "I'm sorry," the nurse said, as she backed down. "That was inappropriate and unprofessional, and you're right. I apologize."

You live alone and die alone. Sheila had said that ruefully on many occasions. She didn't share the risks of her illness or expect her family to rally around her. She appreciated it when it happened but she didn't look to be the center of attention. That nurse probably hadn't ever met anyone like her, someone who was willing to face the likelihood of death head on, alone, without self-pity.

It was a long road to recovery, but Sheila was determined to get back to health as quickly as she could, and to resume her active life again.

Through the late summer and fall of 1987, and into early 1988, Sheila's focus was on rebuilding her strength. She continued her walks around the neighbourhood, a bit longer each day, and a bit more briskly, swinging her arms and breathing deeply. She had to be careful about what she ate, sticking to softer foods as her body healed from the surgery, and she made sure she had her allotment of Ensure every day. She counted her vitamins and took her medications, and an occasional shot of whiskey. She rested. She read. She was upbeat, but bored, and anxious to get back to her studies.

CHAPTER 23
THREE SCORE AND TEN:
1989

One year!

Sheila turned over another page of the calendar and mentally congratulated herself on her one-year postsurgical milestone. It had been a long recovery, but she was feeling much stronger and was itching to get back to her university studies. She had survived her second, very serious, bout of cancer and wanted to put all that behind her. Her degree was within sight, and she would be graduating next year, the spring of 1989. After ten years, she was looking forward to "mission accomplished!" So close to the finish line, she decided to look beyond the Aboriginal Studies list and found that the History Department was offering a course on WW2. The idea intrigued her. *That sounds like fun. Why not?* she told herself. *I know I'm old if my own life has become history, and I'm going to study something I took part in!*

Sheila appeared to have bounced back, just as she had after breast cancer, and while she wasn't yet at 100% of her old self, there was no indication that she wouldn't live a long, long time. She was happy to be back at school and to have a purpose in life again. There was determination and more of a spring in her step on her daily walks. If she knew the survival rates after esophageal cancer, she didn't talk about it.

In fact, the prognosis is poor. If surgery successfully removes all the cancer cells and it hasn't spread elsewhere, there's a 50% chance of living five years. If it has spread, that statistic drops in half, to 25%. Sheila chose not to dwell on the medical facts, preferring to believe she was in the lucky group who survives. She carried on as if cancer was over and done, and as usual shared nothing with Brownie or her kids. The only person who understood how tenuous Sheila's survival chances were was her older sister Kathleen, who was a nurse and knew the odds. "Let me know how your mother is, will you please?" she wrote to Simonne late in 1988. "I worry about her."

It was not long after Kathleen's letter, on a warm spring afternoon in March 1989, when the truth came out. Simonne had dropped in to see Sheila and Brownie and was looking forward to a quick cup of tea, a chat, and the pleasure of having them all to herself for an hour or so. Sheila had recently celebrated her seventieth birthday and all the cards from well-wishers were still on display on the top of the china cabinet. As sunshine poured through the front window they sat in the living room, Brownie slouched on one end of the couch, very quiet and tired looking, not at all himself. Sheila was sitting on the other end, her mug of tea untouched on the coffee table in front of her. She leaned forward and looked directly in Simonne's eyes.

"I have something to tell you," Sheila said, "so I'm glad you popped by today." She was very calm, almost matter-of-fact. "I have cancer again."

"What!? But how?" Simonne asked. "I thought you'd fully recovered from the last bout. Where is it this time? Do you have to have surgery again?" This new development was worrisome, but not alarming. Her mother always bounced back.

Sheila looked over at Brownie. He had his head down as if he didn't want to be part of this conversation. She looked back at Simonne and took a deep breath before speaking.

"It's in my lymph system," she said in a quiet voice. "So that means it's everywhere." And then she looked away, shifting her gaze to the sunny window.

"I'm dying."

It seemed like Sheila had rehearsed this announcement, and she delivered it quickly with a clear voice and dry eyes. Her old explanation *It's just routine* wasn't going to cut it this time. *I must be the first one to hear this, the guinea pig for the bad news,* Simonne realized. *If I hadn't dropped in today, when was she going to tell me? And how is she going to tell Randy, Scott, and Holly?* It was clear Sheila had prepared herself to deliver this bombshell with as little emotion as possible. Brownie knew and now Simonne recognized he was not just subdued, but overwhelmed and broken. The three of them sat unspeaking as the seconds dragged by, and then Simonne finally, awkwardly, broke the silence.

"How long? How much time . . . how much time do you have Mom? Do *we* have?"

"Six, maybe nine, months," Sheila replied. "Less than a year." She took a deep breath. "It's like the Bible says, three score and ten. I'm seventy now. I've had my three score and ten, and so that's it, I guess." The quintessential Sheila stiff upper lip was replaced with a twinge of anger in her voice. She looked away for a moment and then back at Simonne. "Be a lamb and put the kettle on for more tea. Mine's gone cold."

Sheila never put a name on the disease that was destroying her, but lymphoma is the generic term for cancer of the lymph system. It can affect not just the lymph glands, but also the spleen, thymus gland, and bone marrow, as well as other organs like the liver and lungs. Sheila had had some of her lymph glands removed years before as part of her radical mastectomy, a precautionary measure against the breast cancer spreading further. Unfortunately, she also had all three of the major risk factors. She had had previous cancer treatment, had been exposed to radiation after her breast cancer, and had a weakened immune system from her recent surgery. In addition, even though she had quit a long time ago, she had been a smoker for many years. If family history played a part, she was following the pattern set by several of her older siblings who had died in their fifties and sixties from cancer.

Sheila never raised the possibility of treatment.

Despite the devastating finality of her diagnosis, through the rest of the spring, Sheila carried on as if her window of survival was wide open. It was convenient to pretend her life was normal. Even though she was getting thinner and was more fatigued, she remained positive. Her full attention and limited energy was focused on finishing at Trent, and she kept pushing ahead to that goal. She didn't dwell on what was going to happen after graduation.

As she neared the final confirmation that she would be awarded her degree, Sheila began to plan her graduation celebration, and it was going to include all her children and grandchildren. Her gown and cap were pressed, ready and waiting on the hook on the back of the bedroom door, and she splurged on a new dress, unlikely to ever be worn again. All the nicer outfits in her closet were now much too big for her, and she didn't want to look like she was wearing someone else's clothes, someone healthier. She had her hair done by her neighbor/hairdresser, and even agreed to a little makeup. Her grad photo had been taken a few months earlier when her face was still a bit fuller, and was proudly on display in the dining room. She prepared her own announcement for the graduation page in the Peterborough Examiner, mentioning Brownie as if he had organized it. *"Brownie Eccles is proud to announce the graduation of his wife Sheila from Trent University,"* it read, and Brownie *was* proud under his sadness. She reserved a big table for the family at the banquet after the graduation ceremony, adamant that all her children and their spouses attend. "It's my treat!" she insisted happily, refusing any offers to help pay for the tickets. It was Sheila's long awaited big day.

June 2nd, 1989 dawned a beautiful, sunny spring day, without a cloud in the sky, twenty degrees Celsius, the perfect weather for an outdoor convocation in the Trent tradition. Sheila's family took up an entire row of seats in the bleachers set up on the concrete steps outside the university library. They were all there, Randy and Cathy with their children Ryan and Craig, Holly and Andy with Colin and Andrea, Scott and Laurie with Josh and Jade,

Simonne and Guy with Michael, Christy, and Claire. Even Kathleen had come from New Hampshire to help celebrate. The grandkids fidgeted in their stiff shoes and fancy clothes, the whole group lined up like ducklings in a row. Sheila was with the other graduates, waiting off to the side for her name to be called. She was nervous and excited, a little light-headed and afraid at the last minute that she wouldn't be strong enough to walk the long distance across the stage and down the stairs back to her seat. She insisted that Brownie wait with her, insurance in case she needed someone to support her arm at the last minute. He was seated beside the much younger students, uncomfortable in his suit and tie, unsure in this strange and unfamiliar situation, feeling totally out of place and afraid he would do something inappropriate to embarrass them both.

The chancellor began the ceremony by running through the usual welcomes. For the sake of time management, he asked the audience to hold their applause for individuals until each entire class had finished. Sheila's gang sat and watched impatiently as dozens of other graduates came up to the podium to receive their degree and shake the chancellor's hand. There was a smattering of applause now and then and an occasional cheer but most of the audience respected the instructions.

Finally, it was time for Sheila's class. She stood up, waiting in the queue for her name to be called, inching closer and closer as the line of students moved forward. Brownie stood awkwardly off to one side, waiting to be told what to do. Finally, the Chancellor announced "Sheila Eccles!" and without hesitation she began her walk forward. It was immediately obvious she was going to do this by herself without any help, wanting nothing to distract from her success. Brownie needn't have worried. She gave a shake of her head and a firm motion with her hand for him to stay where he was, and with perfect military posture she marched, shoulders back and head high, across the stage. It mimicked almost exactly the way she had demonstrated her army pay parade so many times to her young children, without the snappy salute at the end. She was beaming. Brownie stood at the back of the stage for a moment, then quietly exited from the side. For anyone who didn't know her, Sheila was just an older, very dignified woman happy to get her degree, not someone terminally ill achieving a lifetime goal. Perhaps people wondered why there was an older man with her and why he left the stage. Most likely the audience didn't even notice.

Her children and grandchildren obediently did as they had been asked, not wanting to embarrass her. They sat politely and quietly while they witnessed Sheila's achievement. Even though they really wanted to, they didn't applaud or cheer as she accepted her scroll, or stand up and yell "whoop whoop" as if she had scored the winning goal. They missed their opportunity to publicly hail all that Sheila had accomplished and overcome. It was hard to shout with a big lump in their throats, and a cheer might very well have erupted into a giant sob.

It was a bittersweet day for her family, but a lifetime triumph for Sheila.

Sheila receiving her degree, June 1989. Note the red shoes!
Brownie is waiting with her purse (lower far right).

Back row (left to right): Randy, Scott
Front row (left to right): Holly, Sheila, Brownie, Simonne
Graduation Day.

The whole family including Sheila's sister Kathleen (bottom right).
Missing: Guy and Scott taking pictures, Scott's son Josh.

CHAPTER 24
THE FINAL DAYS:
AUTUMN 1989

The rising tension between Sheila and Brownie exploded after her graduation. Without the distraction of her university studies and feeling increasingly ill, Sheila became more and more angry. It had been easier for her to deny her impending death while she was focused on her degree, but all that was ahead of her now were numbered days and waiting. Their pleasant co-existence over the last years dissolved. Brownie was very stressed, and depressed, and unable to provide the kind of emotional support Sheila needed. He didn't know what he was supposed to say. Nonetheless, as her physical strength declined, the role of the primary caregiver fell on his shoulders. Sheila resented his good health and was critical of the help he tried to provide.

"You all think your father is such a wonderful man," Sheila said bitterly, one day to Simonne. The comment came totally out of the blue. Sheila was standing looking out the front window, agitated, her arms tightly crossed over her chest and her back to the room. Brownie had taken the opportunity to escape somewhere for a moment's respite, to his shed or his garden. "Well, he isn't!" she snapped when she didn't get a response. Simonne continued to say nothing. She knew her father wasn't perfect by a long shot, but she wondered what all this was about..

Back in March 1987, Sheila's oldest sister Agnes had passed away, and although she had never married, she had a daughter, Patricia, from a relationship in the 1930s. She had arranged for her child to be adopted by a well-off couple she knew, and this episode had remained more or less a family secret until Patricia and Agnes reunited years later. Patricia was the beneficiary of Agnes's life insurance policy, but she was not included in Agnes's will. It directed that all of Agnes's substantial assets were to be distributed to her siblings. She had always been generous in her support of the large O'Carroll clan.

Within days of Agnes's funeral, her daughter challenged the will, beginning a long and protracted legal battle to grab the entire estate. When the dust finally settled two years later, during which time Sheila had undergone her cancer surgery and recuperation, she and her two sisters were left with only a small fraction of what Agnes had intended. They were frustrated and angry at the betrayal, and sad that they were not able to carry out their older sister's carefully-made plans.

Sheila received her share in the spring of 1989 at the same time she got the news that she had just months to live. She opened a bank account in her name only and deposited the cheque.

"I know what he'll do with my money," she spat out, as her one-sided rant about Brownie continued. "He'll waste it! He could never handle money. He'll fritter it away on something stupid." She was bitter that it would be Brownie, not she, who benefitted from the gift from *her* cherished sister, much as he had benefitted from Agnes's generous loan for his farm.

Throughout the summer of 1989, as Sheila's health continued to decline, visiting her could be an unsettling experience. It was hard to know what to expect. While she always welcomed a chat, it was rarely about her, how she felt, or if she was afraid, or about the unacknowledged elephant in the room:

Death. More often than not, she danced around discussion of the obvious. Occasionally, though, there were glimpses of how she really felt.

"None of you understand!" Sheila yelled at Simonne one day, no longer able to contain her agitation and frustration at the unfairness of her situation. She needed someone or something, to blame. Or someone to listen. Fists clenched, she was pacing the living room, moving from chair back to chair back for support. A black cloud had descended over the room.

From her armchair, Simonne watched her mother helplessly, stunned at the sudden outburst, and unable to find the right words to comfort either of them. "Don't you think I would fix this if I could?" she finally whispered, her voice cracking and tears threatening to spill. Sheila immediately stopped moving and looked at her daughter in surprise. "Okay," she said softly, dry eyed, taking a breath to steady herself, and then she dropped into a chair. Mother and daughter sat uncomfortably for a moment in silence and then moved on to a safer subject, grandchildren or the weather.

When the focus was on happier things, visits to Sheila and Brownie were much better. "Is there anything of mine you'd like for a keepsake?" she asked Simonne one day as they shared lunch in the kitchen. The question came out of the blue and Simonne had to put her sandwich down for fear of choking on the lump in her throat. They were stepping on very fragile ground. "I've always admired the cameo," Simonne suggested. "I love the story that Dad originally bought it for his mother when he was in Sicily, but then he met you." Brownie turned with a big smile from the counter where he was cleaning plates. Sheila's face lit up too. For a second something unspoken passed between them. The admiration of this special gift seemed to brighten their day, and they were both happy and proud to be able share this little piece of their history. "Go and fetch my jewelry case from on top of the dresser," Sheila instructed. It was a small brown wooden box she had brought with her from England. As a child, Simonne, and later Holly, had tiptoed into her room many times to sneak a look at the treasures inside.

Mostly there were pieces of old costume jewelry from the 30s and 40s, bracelets and necklaces Sheila had worn before the war or when she and Brownie were dressed up for something special. There was a locket with

MIZPAH carved on the back, an old Hebrew word meaning "may the Lord watch over us while we're apart". There was also a very old gold broach with tiny diamonds and a small emerald in its center. It had belonged to Sheila's mother, and before that to her grandmother Sarah Jane Leuttit, and maybe to another generation before that. Sheila's mother Nellie had given it to her just before she left Coventry for Canada. Sheila never wore it, but kept it carefully wrapped in a piece of soft cotton.

"You should have all of this," Sheila said happily. "You're the oldest daughter. Pass it along to your daughters one day, please." Brownie looked on as Sheila and Simonne went through the items in the box, his eyes shining from memories or perhaps tears. Her wedding and engagement rings were there too. "Please take these," she said. "I haven't been able to wear them for a long time because my fingers are so thin and they slide right off."

"Oh, Mom," Simonne whispered. "I couldn't."

"Did I ever tell you about the time I lost them?" Sheila added, trying to lighten the moment. "It was before we had turn signals on cars. I was driving home from the Overseas Club one night, and when I put my arm out the window to make a sign that I was turning, my rings went flying off into the ditch! Your father and a neighbor went back the next morning and searched for ages through all the long grass until they found them. It was a miracle they did." Brownie shook his head and laughed at the memory. "I don't know how we were able to find just the right place to look," he said. "We were lucky."

"They're just cheap war-time gold. Precious metals were hard to find back then," Sheila added apologetically, holding them out, "but maybe you could do something with them."

Simonne took them gently from Sheila's hand. "I'll treasure them."

These old pieces, trinkets and baubles, were worth very little in the monetary sense, but they were markers in Sheila's life, symbols of past times and happiness.

It was a chilly day in early October when Simonne made another impromptu visit, checking in for a quick hello, as usual in a hurry. "I've gotta go, Mom," she said after an hour or so, putting on her coat in the entry way just a few steps below the living room. "I've got to get home to the kids."

"Wait a minute," Sheila said, slowly pulling herself up from her armchair. "Brownie, help me." She had become even more thin and weak, but with his support she walked slowly to the stairs and held the railing at the top. She was no longer able to come out to the driveway for her traditional extended goodbye and last minute comments, so she was going to make them here in the foyer. As Simonne leaned in to kiss her mother on the cheek, Sheila reached out and took her oldest daughter's face in both her hands. She said nothing for a moment, but looked deeply into her eyes, as if to convey a message she couldn't verbalize.

"Goodbye, I'll see you soon. I'll be back in a week or so if I can," Simonne said, pulling away from her mother's hands and feeling a bit disconcerted at the intensity of their interaction.

"Bye-bye," Sheila said softly, still smiling, her dark eyes shining. "Drive carefully. Please give my love to all your lovely kiddies."

Sheila knew it was their last farewell.

Holly had planned to make the long trip again from Cochrane the first weekend in November. "We'll be there to see you next Saturday," she said on the phone to Sheila a week before. "No, you'll be here to see your father," Sheila replied. Holly corrected her, a bit puzzled. "I'm coming to see *you*. Andy too, and we're bringing the kids. We're leaving Saturday," she repeated. "No, you'll see your father," Sheila insisted again, firmly. *She's confused,* Holly thought. *What's she talking about?*

The last few days of that October were unusually warm, sunny days with a temperature around 20 Celsius. Sheila had always loved the fresh air of autumn and the glorious colours of the falling leaves, so she asked Brownie to carry her outside to sit in a lawn chair at the end of the driveway. She stayed there for the afternoon, with a blanket around her, soaking up the last rays of warm sunshine and saying hello to the neighbours walking by. Or perhaps she was saying goodbye.

Sheila passed away quietly two days later, on Monday, October 30th, 1989. She didn't know that Randy, Scott, and Simonne were at her bedside with Brownie and Kathleen. Holly had made it only as far as North Bay by the time Sheila died.

She was finally at rest, no more battles to wage. She died on her own terms, dignified and without fanfare. She was seventy years old.

* * * * * * * * *

Having learned from the experience of Agnes's estate problems, Sheila took steps to get her own affairs in order. Just a few weeks before she died she arranged for a lawyer to visit the house. She met with him in private, barring Brownie from any discussion or any joint estate planning. The only thing she did share with him, after things were finalized, was the plan for her funeral. She had contacted a funeral home and paid in advance for cremation and a simple service in their chapel, even providing the single picture she wanted displayed. It was her university graduation photo. She had chosen a niche for her ashes, and Brownie's when the time came, at the memorial gardens across the highway from their old pink and white house. They would be in the granite wall that faced the road. She had always said that would be a good place to be left. "I can watch the cars coming and going," she'd joked.

As she had for her graduation dinner, Sheila had planned and coordinated every detail of her funeral in advance, outlined in a neat folder left on her desk. All her family had to do was to show up. She had saved them the pain of trying, and possibly failing, to determine what she might have wanted. She had deftly avoided difficult discussions, heavy with emotions. It was her final attempt to have some control over a battle she had already lost.

As if Sheila's graduation a few months earlier had been a dress rehearsal for the funeral, everyone was there in their best clothes, lined up, shaking hands and accepting condolences at the funeral home. Fellow students and old work colleagues came to pay their respects, as did most of the neighbours, and all the Eccles family. The Millbrook Legion sent a delegation to honour Sheila's military service. Her sister Kathleen, who had been with her in her last days, was present as the O'Carroll representative.

"Sheila was such a wonderful person," the family was told again and again.

"She was so interested in life."

"Such a great listener."

"Sheila was an inspiration."

"She always had a moment to chat."

"Your mother was a fascinating woman," a dignified gentleman said to Randy and Simonne as he introduced himself. "I'm Professor Robson, one of Sheila's Trent professors. I'm not sure why she chose me, but I'm honored to give her eulogy."

The class Sheila had taken from him was the history of WW2, the one she had signed up for "just for fun," and he had encouraged her to write about her own experiences in the war. Initially she had balked at the idea. "I don't like to look back," she had told him, but with his encouragement she returned to those important years in her life.

"I truly enjoyed the experience of having her in my history class. In fact, truth be told, Sheila taught me. We shared a real love of history and I felt as though she took me back with her in time."

"Sheila's essay was very good," Professor Robson said, "and as I read about the people and events Sheila recalled, I discovered a familiar face, a friend, in the different country that is the past." Behind the wrinkled face of the terminally ill seventy year old, Professor Robson saw the young woman. He ended the eulogy by describing that girl in one word. "She was plucky," he said. It was a wartime term that fit her perfectly.

With the official, sad part done, Sheila had also organized a reception at the house after the funeral, with lots of food to serve the guests and a good supply of alcohol on hand. She had thought of all the details, she who avoided funerals and didn't organize parties. *The Eccles will all need a drink,* she predicted accurately. *And they may want to play cards later in the evening.* Sheila hated card games, and could never understand the attraction, but she knew her in-laws well. In anticipation, she had bought new decks of playing cards bearing the Trent University crest. They were at the ready in their clean new boxes on the dining room dresser.

The post-funeral party proved a roaring success. The food was plentiful and excellent and the drinks flowed, just as she had intended. There were more laughs than tears, and for the first time in weeks Brownie, though exhausted and overwhelmed, was smiling.

Sheila was no doubt looking on somehow, enjoying the fun, proud of the success of her last hurrah.

There were so many times that day when one of Sheila's children thought, *Wait until I tell Mom about this*, or caught themselves before they said out loud, *Mom's going to love that story*. And then they remembered.

When everyone had gone home and the remains of the party were cleared away, Randy, Holly, and Simonne, with their spouses and kids, had to go back to their everyday lives miles away. Only Scott was left in Peterborough to check in on Brownie. Kathleen returned to the States. Her companionship and support in Sheila's final days had been a gift of love. Brownie's favorite sister Evelyn stayed with him for a few days after the funeral, but she too had her own life to get on with, and soon Brownie was left on his own. He was a shell of the person he had been seven months earlier, thin and grey-looking, and at a loss about what to do next.

He hated being alone in their house, now empty of Sheila except for her medications and toiletries in the bathroom and her clothes in the closet. Despite the tension between them as she was dying, he missed her being there.

"I think something bad must have happened to Sheila that she wouldn't tell me about," he confided to Simonne. "She was angry. I asked her but she refused to say anything."

"She was frustrated by what *didn't* happen, Dad," Simonne told him. "She wasn't ready to die when she still had so much more living to do."

Brownie went on to live for almost two more decades. In his final days, his memories of Sheila were only good ones. "I still miss her," he said often. "Sheila was always so much fun."

He didn't get to see her 1986 letter and know that she had been happy (mostly) with her life.

Hey God, thanks a lot, it was a good day! He/she has been good to me. Not in all things, but in most.

Sheila (O'Carroll) Eccles, age seventy.

EULOGY
SHEILA ECCLES

NOVEMBER 1ST, 1989
BY PROFESSOR STUART ROBSON, TRENT UNIVERSITY

I knew Sheila for less than a year when she took my course last year on the history of the Second World War. But travelers can get to know each other in a special way that has nothing to do with the clock, and Sheila and I traveled together, even though we did not leave my office.

For Sheila, it was a voyage into her own past.

When I first suggested that she write about Britain in the war by concentrating on her own experience, she was reluctant. She said she did not like to look back. But she agreed to give it a try, and as the year unfolded, I had the privilege of hearing about what she called the "Postings, Places and People" of O'Carroll, Sheila, W/22123, her number in the British Women's Royal Army Corps. So it was a voyage for me as well.

Her first term essay was very good, and as I read the people and events Sheila recalled, I discovered a familiar face, a friend, in the different country that is the past. Obviously, she not only retrieved a lot of valuable memories when she looked back, but she was able to make sense of what she had experienced. For her, as for us all, remembering was a form of therapy, a way of coming to terms with what has happened to us.

The jokes she remembered from the Blitz were especially good. She told me about the elderly couple who were blown clear out of their flat. When the wife was asked if she was all right, she replied, "Oh yes, it's the first time we've been out together in years." She told me about her apprehension when she told her Irish father she was joining the British Army. "That's all right, Sheila," he replied, "all the best British generals are Irish," a boast that happens to be true.

She recalled her disappointment when she was assigned to the Pay Corps, and her keenness on later becoming a messenger and ambulance driver for the Army. She told me how the discipline she had learned had helped her in later life. When physiotherapy had been especially difficult, she drew upon her training in marching and parading. She showed me how to parade, shoulders braced and back erect, and I saw her as she had been forty years back. Even her army boots were part of the story. She said that when one of her daughters was taunted at school with the ancient cry "Your mother wears army boots," the daughter replied "Yes, she wears them for gardening." Why not, Sheila asked, they were excellent leather.

She told me how she met her husband, and how she adjusted as a war bride.

You knew her as a woman who was a wife, and a mother, and dear friend, but I had the good fortune to get to know the girl as well. The wonderful qualities we have gathered to remember were in her all along. When Sheila was a teenager, the English novelist E.M. Forster described the people he admired, the people who kept the chance of civilization alive. I happen to share his view, and I think it applies to Sheila.

I believe in aristocracy, though—if that is the right word, and if a democrat may use it. Not an aristocracy of power, based on rank and influence, but an aristocracy of the sensitive, the considerate, and the plucky. Its members are to be found in all nations and classes, and all through the ages, and there is a secret understanding between them when they meet. They represent the true human

condition, the one permanent victory of our queer race over cruelty and chaos . . .
. They are sensitive for others without being fussy, their pluck is not swankiness but
the power to endure, and they can take a joke.

In the sense Forster meant, I took a trip with someone special. It was a
voyage I will not forget. All of us were privileged to travel a while with Sheila.

ACKNOWLEDGEMENTS

Writing the story of my mother's life was a journey through the twentieth century, a ride on an emotional rollercoaster, and most importantly, an opportunity to meet an adult friend. Sheila.

The details of her story were found in the boxes and boxes of Sheila's memorabilia, including unmailed letters in which she shared her most private thoughts, but then didn't have the confidence to drop in the mailbox. Some of the anecdotes came from my own experiences, and others from the stories shared by my siblings and cousins. Despite my best efforts, there will be errors because that's what happens with oral history. It bends over time. Most of the dialogue I've included is as accurate as I could make it from my memory, and some is my best approximation of Sheila's voice and what others probably said. All of the letters I've quoted are real.

When I started this project I wrote about Sheila from the perspective of a daughter, but as I learned more about the parts of her life I hadn't shared, I began to discover a different person. I was finally able to see the complex, imperfect, unconventional woman she was. She surprised and delighted me, made me laugh and made me cry.

Thank you to all the contributors to Sheila's story: my brothers Randy and Scott and my sister Holly, for opening your hearts and trusting me. I hope I haven't disappointed you. To my cousin Michael O'Carroll, who made a huge contribution to dates and times but sadly died before I was done. To cousins Ruth, Nora, Trisha, and Gail for your wonderful O'Carroll stories. The information from all of you has been so helpful and I hope you'll overlook any misinterpretations. To my writing coach Nora Zylstra-Savage for urging me on, and to my friends Marion and Arthur, who read my manuscript and gave me the confidence to go forward.

Finally thank you to my wonderful husband Guy whose love of WW2 history and fascination about all things Irish provided the context, and who never lost faith that I would eventually finish. How I wish you were here to help me celebrate the final product.

And of course, thank you Mom. I still miss you.

Simonne Ferguson

Lightning Source UK Ltd.
Milton Keynes UK
UKHW010122011222
413111UK00006B/910